ENLIGHTENMENT IS

NOT

WHAT YOU THINK

Also by
Wayne (Ram Tzu) Liquorman:

NO WAY for the Spiritually "Advanced"

Acceptance of What IS...a book about Nothing

Never Mind

ENLIGHTENMENT IS NOT WHAT YOU THINK

THE LIVING TEACHING OF
WAYNE LIQUORMAN

EDITED BY DAWN SALVA

TRANSCRIBED BY JOHN STRYDOM

Advaita Press

Published in the USA by

Advaita Press
PO Box 3479
Redondo Beach, CA 90277
Tel: 310-376-9636
Email: fellowship@advaita.org
www.advaita.org

Cover Design : Sandra Llanas

Rear Cover Photo: Gayle Goodrich

ISBN-10: 0-929448-22-7
ISBN-13: 978-0-929448-22-0

Library of Congress Card Number: 2009924920

10-9-8-7-6-5-4-3-2-1

With gratitude to the Balsekars
For welcoming me in

Peace of mind is the only true happiness. All the rest is merely misery in disguise.

Tukaram

CONTENTS

What is Enlightenment?—Arising of the FSA—Getting Rid of Ego—The Body Stays—Can We Know the Truth?—A Higher State—Relativity—Experience of The Sage—Feeling Enlightened—Experience of Enlightenment—Enlightened Conduct—Self-Consciousness—Genuinely Enlightened—Who Gets Enlightened?

Who is Steering the Boat?—Taking Life Personally—No Self—Describing Consciousness—Who is Permanently Beyond?—Presence is Personal Experience—Programmed to See—Cause and Effect—All is Consciousness—Transcendence—Wanting Absence, Seeking Presence—What is Being Sought?—Grace—Spiritual Experiences—Manifestation

Meditation—Being Still—Be Earnest, Be Sincere—Letting Go—Spiritual Practices—Living in the Moment—Doing Nothing—Is There Nothing For Me to Do?—Effort, Prayer and Predestination—Finding the Right Formula—Perceiver and Perceived—Karma—Reincarnation—Practices—Religion— Guru and Disciple—Which Teachings? Whose Choice?—Who is Asking the Questions?—Who is Resisting?—Who is Seeking?—Ending the Seeking—It's All a Dream—Subject and Object—Pointers as Tools—Waiting to Get it Over With

EDITOR'S NOTE

There are thousands of courses, books, religions and philosophies offering methods to gain success, peace, even Enlightenment. This is not one of them. It is, however, an opportunity to hear, and perhaps experience Wisdom with a contemporary, living sage, one in whom the event called Enlightenment has happened.

This collection of questions, answered by Wayne Liquorman, is extracted from volumes of "sessions" attended by people from around the world. It is transcribed, for the most part, from live recordings, in Q & A format. Not only does Wayne clarify numerous misconceptions about Enlightenment, but frankly, and often quite humorously, he addresses questions ranging from emotions and thoughts, to global issues and spirituality.

Ironically, as a successful California businessman and a recovering alcoholic, Wayne had no prior interest in spirituality, much less a desire to become a spiritual teacher. Various life events happened and Wayne was led to meet his beloved guru, Ramesh Balsekar, culminating in Wayne's "Living Teaching" in the Advaita tradition as exemplified in this collection.

This book is "alive" as few spiritual books can be. Although words can only point to the indescribable Source, Wayne's personality—so full of humor, love, and patience—flows through these words with a profound Wisdom. Both the delightful Wayne and this treasured collection of insights are surprisingly accessible, thoroughly enjoyable, and an invaluable resource for the curious.

Dawn Salva

TRANSCRIBER'S NOTE

Some years ago fate assigned to me the task of transcribing and editing some of Wayne Liquorman's talks. I wanted to make some contribution towards supporting his teaching and I hoped I would learn more effectively if I took the time to write down his words, one by one. During this process I found myself becoming increasingly drawn to some of the more perplexing aspects of his teachings as I puzzled through those many words over hundreds of hours, covering some forty talks. He said, again and again, in his responses to students' questions - many of which I shared - that his words would find their mark to the degree to which one was able to receive them in the spirit in which they were intended.

He repeatedly emphasized that his words were mere pointers to the seemingly elusive goal, and that I, as I currently conceived of myself, could not become enlightened. So when I started "getting it" - after many misunderstandings and wishful re-interpretations - I was by turns surprised, dismayed and appalled at this seemingly discouraging news.

But I had to admit that I had heard similar statements before from many other teachers; what he had to say could be encapsulated in the Zen notion that what there is - and the I is not there - is already enlightened, and in Nisargadatta Maharaj's assertion that not even one more experience is necessary for enlightenment to be present. Centuries of such strange speaking have gone before, and spiritual teachers aver that such paradoxical teaching is all that is possible as long as words have to be used. It was I who needed to hear again, and more deeply, what I had not truly been able to hear before, but this time the message was expressed in Wayne's inimitably humorous and provocative style.

Wayne's teaching is part of the alluring and enduring tradition of spiritual enquiry in which the question is always more important than the answer, and in which the love and immeasurable patience of the teacher are what heal the wounds of the seeker. His humorous and gentle chipping away at my preconceptions continue to be a tremendous comfort during the hard times and I trust the same will be the case for those who are blessed to read between the lines and behind his words. The impersonal Love will be found there, whatever personal angle one is coming from.

John Strydom
Mooinooi, South Africa

INTRODUCTION

Through a series of circumstances, clearly not of my own making, I have found myself cast in the role of a spiritual teacher. As a result, for the last ten years or so I have been invited by interested people and groups from around the world to speak about that of which it is not possible to speak. It is a peculiar job but no odder, I suppose, than being the one responsible for removing pigeon droppings from the statues in the square or etching the Lotus Sutra onto a grain of rice.

One of the topics I am often questioned about when I speak is Enlightenment. The questions themselves are quite revealing. It is clear that there is an enormous store of misinformation and fantasy surrounding the subject. Should you be moved to continue reading this book you will find a representative sampling of the kinds of things people ask about Enlightenment. My answers, though varied, always seem to boil down to a single pointer:

Rather than being the presence of something, Enlightenment is the absence of something.

The logical next question is, "What is this something that is absent?" Here is where we move from the realm of relative knowledge and science (where we tend to be comfortable) into the amorphous realm of the Mystic (where we are often quite uncomfortable). The realm of the Mystic is therefore a less inviting place to linger and most people never venture there. I have given this "something" that is absent in Enlightenment (which you may discover to be Nothing) a name: The False Sense of Authorship

(FSA for short). The False Sense of Authorship is an admittedly cumbersome term and will often be replaced with the acronym FSA through the course of this book. Over the years I have tried various other terms—the "me", the ego, the Thinking Mind to name but a few—and all have revealed themselves as containing the seeds of considerable misunderstanding and confusion. So it seems that, at least for the moment, we are both stuck with False Sense of Authorship (FSA) to point to that which is absent in the human being we say is Enlightened.

Since you are reading these lines it is fair to assume that you have at least a passing interest in this subject of Enlightenment. My questions to you then are: "What is it you imagine Enlightenment to be? If you were to obtain Enlightenment what do you imagine your life would then be like?"

I urge you to stop reading for a moment and give this a bit of thought.

Hopefully the dialogues on the following pages will help to dispel some of the more debilitating fantasies relating to Enlightenment and Enlightened beings. If you jot down some of your thoughts about the questions above and then read them again when you finish this book you may be surprised to see how your understanding has changed. Who knows? You might even find the process itself to be Enlightening…

Wayne Liquorman
Hermosa Beach
March 2009

ACKNOWLEDGMENTS

Many people worked long and hard to make this book a reality. John Strydom did most of the heavy lifting in the initial transcriptions and organization, and then Dawn Salva applied her considerable talents as an editor to mold this into something that I hope will find a home in the hearts and minds of at least a few interested readers.

Dawn, John and Michael Islander did the proof-reading...which is useful information when laying the blame for any errors. Everyone had different ideas about comma placement and I ultimately made the final decisions based firmly on whimsy.

I am particularly grateful for the ongoing support of Steven Hoel and Nacho Fagalde... two of the biggest and most generous hearts I have been privileged to know.

My wife, Jaki, made several very valuable suggestions that have found their way onto these pages. But most importantly, her love and support provides the fuel that keeps me moving.

My greatest measure of gratitude goes, as always, to my guru, Ramesh Balsekar. His patience and love over the last twenty plus years has been unwavering despite the appalling way I have mangled his teaching.

~~~

SECTION ONE: ENLIGHTENMENT

WHAT IS ENLIGHTENMENT?

Q: What do you mean by Enlightenment?"

Wayne: When I talk about Enlightenment, I talk about it very, very specifically, and it's extremely simple. In humans, at around the age of two-and-a-half, a profound shift occurs in which we change from spontaneous, free-flowing beings, to creatures in which everything is about "Me!" and "Mine!" and how to get what "I" want and think "I" need. It is the moment that the false sense of personal author-ship (FSA) starts. It happens to virtually every human being. It is the false sense that "I", as this body-mind organism, am the source that makes things happen.

It is this false sense of authorship that creates suffering, because the new perception is that "I" am in control of things. Yet there is continuous evidence to the contrary—that "I" am not in control. So a powerful tension is established.

Later, for some people, for whatever reason, that sense of personal authorship permanently dissolves. We can say it dies. That event is called Enlightenment. Over the millennia, people have mystified the hell out of it. Basically, it's an event that happens in the history of some human organisms.

The reason this event is so interesting to some people is that after Enlightenment, the human organism is no longer suffering. There is Total Acceptance within the organism. There is Total Acceptance because it is "understood" that What Is, Is. There is no longer a separate claiming "me" to become involved with What Is, claiming it as "mine."

Q: You still get angry and sad. It just doesn't make you suffer?

Wayne: Exactly! Anger and sadness are simply functions of the human apparatus. Humans are designed to experience a variety of emotions and reactions. Painful experience in itself does not create suffering. What creates suffering is involvement by the False Sense of Authorship in the painful experience. When the separate "me" (FSA) becomes involved in the pain of the moment, it projects the pain into the past or the future, resulting in suffering.

Q: How does Enlightenment happen? How do you return to that state? It just happens?

Wayne: It happens. It happens as part of the functioning of the universe. The pointer of this teaching—that I am calling The Living Teaching—is that everything happens that way; everything happens as part of the functioning of Totality.

~~~

Q: I've heard you say that "the meat does not become Enlightened." What do you mean by this?

Wayne: What I mean is that Enlightenment is transcendent of the body-mind. It is not limited to the physical organism. The physical organism was born and will die. They all do. Nobody gets out of this alive. Enlightenment is not a relative state that comes and goes. It is transcendent of this physical form and is eternal. That's why it's often said, as a pointer by sages, "I"—speaking from the perspective of Transcendence—"was never born, therefore I"—as Transcendence—"will never die, I am not this body, I am not limited to this form."

Q: And so you have had a kind of peek into the eternal?

Wayne: *Who?* You see, now you're thinking in terms of the body/mind again.

Q: Since you are in your body.

Wayne: No, no. *I am not in my body.* That's the whole point. When speaking from the standpoint of Transcendence, I am not *in* the body. I speak *through* the body. The body is a temporary phenomenon. I am the eternal.

Q: So, at this point in your life you have both, actually.

Wayne: Who "has" both? You keep positing a "me"

that is Enlightened, and functioning as the body. What I am saying is that there is no such "me". There is simply the body which functions, and the "I" which functions through it.

Q: And so the "I" is not the "me"?

Wayne: The "I" is not limited to the "me". The "me" is the false claimer of the "I". It's the "me" who falsely claims to be the Source.

~~~

Q: Why are the definitions of Enlightenment different from different masters? Is there anything common among all the definitions?

Wayne: Enlightenment is essentially indescribable. The various definitions, or pointers to Enlightenment, are all relative and they're all limited. That's what they have in common. If you understand them to be poetry, rather than science, then you're way ahead of the game, because you're not looking to compare poems to find out which one is true. So, with the understanding that *none* of the descriptors of Enlightenment are inherently true, you can then go with the one you like, for as long as you like. Then when ready, you can switch to one you like better, until there is no longer a need for descriptions at all.

~~~

Q: What defines the movement of Enlightenment?

Wayne: The total absence of movement. Enlighten-ment is the absence of the movement between the experience of being One, and the experience of be-ing separate. Mystics often say that what is left, when you remove the experience of the unitive and the separate, is Unity, because that's all that *ever* is. It is simply masked by the dualistic movement. The temp-tation is to imagine—and it's reinforced by thousands of years of descriptions of this state by sages—that the sage constantly experiences this unity that seek-ers temporarily experience. This is not the case.

Essentially, what the seeker is looking for is to have a one-sided coin. That fantasy is to only have the side that is the non-dual, or unitive experience, without its converse, the separate experience. It's a very attractive idea. It's very attractive to imagine having the good without the bad, the healthy with-out the sick, and the joy without the sorrow but so far, that's not been the nature of the manifest uni-verse.

As long as we're dealing in this manifest uni-verse, there is no escaping its dualistic structure. What the sage is pointing to is a Transcendence that encompasses the dualistic, manifest universe but is itself, *featureless*. When the sage talks about the Fea-tureless, he can only describe it by means of terms that match the seeker's experience of the unitive state. Then the seeker says, "Aha, I know what that state is, I've been there, I've felt that and I love it. Furthermore, I want to have that *all the time!*"

Q: Right on!

Wayne: Well, you are in luck. There is no shortage of people willing to provide you with a variety of methods to finally achieve that which you want; whether it's a meditative practice, a tantric practice, a yogic practice, or whatever; there are endless practices available, many of which are marketed by promising that you will eventually be in a permanent state of bliss.

What I tend to get here in this room are the burnout cases, who have been through that process over and over and over. I don't get a lot of young people here. Mostly, the people who get here have been around the spiritual block. They've sat on the cushions in every conceivable posture of discomfort, they've had the dysentery, they've been to the ashrams and they've endured all of these things that need to be endured to "attain that which is sought." After they've done that for fifteen, twenty, thirty years, some people will begin to be open to the notion this Living Teaching introduces.

In most cases, the "me" has to take a real slamming. It has to have claimed to have really tried, to have earnestly made the effort to accomplish, to have followed all the instructions, to have done what needed to be done. At some point, the people who get here look up and say, "Hey, I did what they told me to do. I was really earnest. I did what the first guy said and that didn't work out, and then I did what the next guy said and *that* didn't work out, and then I did what the *next* guy said and that didn't work out either; maybe there's a trap in all this!" [laughter]

Q: And I'm pissed because I spent all that time on it!

Wayne: You may well be pissed, but you may also now begin to see that everything that has happened was part of an inescapable process. All those hours on those cushions, all the discomforts, all the hardships, all those gurus, all those things that you've done, were all preparations for the next stage. They were not "wasted," but were part of the unfolding.

Q: What exactly is the process?

Wayne: *This* is the process! You don't need a story about it. When you say, "The process is..." then you've missed the point. We're in the middle of the process. It is going on *now*. You're experiencing the process. You're feeling the process. You are engaged in the process. It isn't happening outside of you, it *is* you. When you name it and contextualize it, you feel removed from it.

ARISING OF THE FSA

Q: You use these terms ego, "me," doer, FSA—my understanding is that it's all Consciousness. The FSA is part of that Consciousness, so it's not a bad thing, a wrong thing, or something to transcend. But still there's this big conversation about getting rid of it.

Wayne: There is indeed. When I talk about the False Sense of Authorship (FSA), I don't think of it as a lower state versus the higher state called Enlightenment. But the FSA is the mechanism through which human suffering happens and this makes it something people want to be rid of.

In my definition, the FSA, in fact, does nothing. Its sole function is to claim the functioning of the Universe as it happens through a particular organism as being "my" doing. When you look into it, it is such a ludicrous claim! It is ridiculous—totally unsupportable. And yet, that profound sense that "I'm" the one responsible for making things happen is a central feature of virtually every human.

Ramesh coined the phrase "Divine hypnosis" to describe this false sense that the "me" has of being the ultimate author. This sense is often present even if the intellect fully acknowledges that it couldn't possibly be the author. That's why the term "Divine hypnosis" is so beautiful. If everything is Divine, if everything is One, then even the presence of the FSA, must be part of that. It's not self-hypnosis; the "me" can't even create that. It may claim that it creates it, but again it's a false claim. It's a false claim of personal authorship.

Q: So even if someone would say, "I just washed my car," within that context you're saying that's perceived as authorship?

Wayne: Not necessarily. It may or may not be perceived as authorship. After Enlightenment someone can say, "I washed my car," and it's a statement as devoid of authorship as "the sun rose at 6:53 this morning." Both are statements of fact. I—this organism—washed the car. That indeed happened.

Q: The difference is?

Wayne: The difference is if this FSA is present to claim the washing of the car, pride may follow. Within that pride is the seed of suffering. Wherever there is pride, guilt is soon to follow.

~~~

Q: Where does the FSA come from?

Wayne: Where it physically comes from and why it arises are questions I can't answer. All I can do is point to the fact that in virtually every human being, at approximately the age of two-and-a-half, this false sense of authorship arises.

Q: So you see it as just a part of the human machinery and if it wasn't for humans, there would be no "me" perception in the universe?

Wayne: I am hard-pressed to say what is happening in the rest of the universe. [laughter] What I can say is that as far as we know, the presence of the FSA is a dubious distinction of humanity. The sense of authorship is uniquely human. When that false sense of authorship later falls away, we call that occurrence Enlightenment. The curious thing about the disappearance of this false notion is that it doesn't change anything. Things remain as they always were.

GETTING RID OF EGO

Q: Can the FSA stay gone?

Wayne: The "stay gone" is the Enlightenment. The coming and going is what we call spiritual experience. What's confusing is that sometimes it's gone for a while, so you may think this is it! But your thinking that "This is it", is not it.

Q: So you should just let go of the "me" and let things happen?

Wayne: Who is going to let go of the "me" and let things happen? It is that illusory "me" which says, "I'm going to let go of "me" and just let things happen. Then everything is going to be great, I'll have mastered this situation."

Q: But in some sense, isn't there an effort to let go of being in control?

Wayne: There may well be some effort exerted in letting go of being in control. Who is exerting the effort?

Q: The "me".

Wayne: The "me" does nothing. It only claims that it is exerting the effort—which is a false claim. The organism, which is a product of the complex forces of the universe, exerts the effort. The exertion comes about as a result of these complex forces of the universe. The "me" then says, "I did that."

Q: But the organism is still doing its thing?

Wayne: Absolutely, it will do things until it is dead. The question as always is, what is the source of the doing?

~~~

Q: How does the dissolution of the "me" come about? Through inquiry?

Wayne: It happens.

Q: It just happens.

Wayne: Not "just" happens. It *happens*.

Q: It happens.

Wayne: Everything happens! That's one of the many things that happen. Then we tell stories about these various happenings, why they happened and how they happened.

Q: How did it happen for you? It happens for each person differently?

Wayne: Yes. Each person's history is different, each person's story is different.

Q: I believe I've experienced that witness and dissolution of it before in my life, and I recognize it. Is it possible that it can come and go?

Wayne: Yes, this coming and going is very much the experience of the seeker—to have moments of presence and impersonal witnessing, followed by moments of separation and involvement. That movement back and forth, in and out of that state, is the condition of the seeker.

Q: That's what I have felt, but that's really not Enlightenment because it hasn't stayed?

Wayne: Enlightenment is the absence of both the experience of the unity and the experience of the separation. What you've experienced is the sense of the separate "me" falling away. Right?

Q: Yes.

Wayne: Life and living, of course, go on; the universe goes on. Then this "me" comes back and looks at that period of unity that is demarcated on the front side by the departure of the "me," and on the back side by the return of the "me," and says, "*That* was it."

Q: That's been my experience.

Wayne: That is the experience of the seeker. And then you say, "I want that all the time."

Q: Exactly! So how can I feel it all the time?

Wayne: "You" cannot feel it all the time; that is the entire point. The fantasy is that when "I" get "it," "I" will know "it" all the time. You have known "it," because "it" became quantified. It had a beginning; it had an end; it was knowable as some *thing*.

What happens to the organism we call the sage is that the identified, involved "me" dies; life and living go on, but there is no "me" to come back and quantify What Is as some thing. So, we can say that the sage does not *know* the Oneness; rather, the sage *is* the Oneness.

Q: But for the sage, does the "me" come back?

Wayne: No. After Enlightenment, the involved "me" is dead and gone. There is nothing to come back and quantify What Is as some thing. Therefore, the sage IS the Oneness and does not *know* or *experience* the Oneness. The seeker is able to experience unity because the experience ends, and so it becomes something quantifiable and knowable. What Is is not knowable unless you are separate from it. Afterwards you quantify "it" as something and then know "it" as Oneness. That whole model is not available any longer for the sage, because that which would come back and quantify, that which would be separate and know the Oneness, is no more.

Q: Obviously, having had intellectual understanding, or even having had the experience of unity as a seeker, we do not remain in that state. Why does the

FSA come back for the seeker and not the sage?

Wayne: For the seeker, the FSA is asleep. In the sage, the FSA is dead.

THE BODY STAYS

Q: After Enlightenment, do you see the body as something that is just there, but you don't identify with it anymore?

Wayne: Identification is a tricky word. You need a *primary* identification so that you are able to function. If you didn't know this was your body, you wouldn't be able to lift the glass to bring it to your mouth; you'd just pour water into your computer instead, because there wouldn't be any difference between you and the computer! This primary, functional identification is essential and it is universal to all human beings.

Sometimes there arises a *secondary* quality to identification that I call "authorship." This is the false claim that what happens through me, the body-mind apparatus, is *my* authored doing, that *I* am the source of the doing. It is the sense that I am an independently creative being who is ultimately responsible for the presence or absence of thoughts, actions and emotions. It is this secondary identification that Enlightenment is concerned with. Enlightenment is the total dissolution of that secondary identification.

After Enlightenment, the sage continues to function and continues to use personal pronouns. He says, "This is my house, this is my family, this is my dog, etc.," and relates things to himself, which he must do in order to function in life. So, the primary identification is there, but the secondary involvement, which claims authorship for "my" thoughts, "my" actions and "my" emotions, is not. It is that secondary involvement, which produces guilt when things go badly or pride if things turn out right. Therefore, pride and guilt can never arise in the sage.

CAN WE KNOW THE TRUTH?

Q: I don't know much about this Living Teaching. Is it a teaching?

Wayne: It is a teaching.

Q: How do you practice? Is it something you can *do*?

Wayne: The Living Teaching begins with the principle that nothing that I say is the Truth.

Q: "Truth" meaning?

Wayne: Ultimate Truth.

Q: Because there is no truth?

Wayne: Because all conceptual truth is relative: somebody is going to agree; somebody is going to disagree. Anything that is said, anything that is taught, is dualistic in nature and can be disputed.

Q: Anything anybody says?

Wayne: Anything anybody says.

Q: Because of the limits of language?

Wayne: Because of the limit of the human mind. The mind is an instrument of duality. What the Living Teaching points to is not dualistic.

Q: Can experience be the Truth?

Wayne: Experience is also dualistic in nature.

Q: So, we can never experience the Absolute, or maybe parts of it only?

Wayne: Everything that is experienced is an aspect of the Truth. In this Living Teaching, we give Truth the name Consciousness—or you may also call it God, Source, Oneness, Unicity, Christ, Tao—it doesn't matter what you call it; these are all pointers to that Totality of which everything is an aspect. So, the Truth can be known in its aspect, but not in its Totality. We are functioning in duality, so we can say within relative duality there are statements that we call either true or false. It must always be remembered that those are relative evaluations, not absolutes. True

Absolute cannot be known, cannot be experienced, except in its aspect, which is the manifest universe.

Perhaps you've had profound experiences of unity or presence. We call that type of experience "spiritual." It has a quality of being total, of being unfettered, unlimited. And yet, if you can know it, if you can experience it, it must be limited. My guru, Ramesh Balsekar, calls those experiences "free samples" or "glimpses over the fence," but they're not Enlightenment. That's what sets this teaching firmly apart from many of the teachings you may have encountered so far. It is saying that the experience of unity is a relative experience; even the profound union with God that one knows is relative and not the ultimate Truth, despite how profound it feels. Even the most profound experience is a temporary aspect of the Total.

~~~

Q: We live in a dualistic world, perceiving in a dualistic manner. How can we get in touch with something that's non-dual?

Wayne: Ahhh, that is the mystery of the mystic and the mystical. The mystic is pointing beyond the relative, and then you're rightly asking, "How can I go beyond the relative?" Any mystic worth his salt will tell you, you *can't*. You absolutely cannot go beyond the relative, and yet the mystic will in the same breath say, "I have gone beyond the relative."

Q: Wouldn't the mystic say that we're all beyond

the relative?

Wayne: That depends on the mystic! [laughter] Because these are all pointers, you see? All of these relative statements are imperfect representations of that which cannot be represented. You can only represent something that exists as an object. What the mystic is pointing at is not an object, it's not a thing.

Q: But then how can we perceive it?

Wayne: You can't perceive it!

Q: Then how can we know about it? That's what I don't see! How can you even talk about it if it can't be perceived, or felt, or understood or looked at?

Wayne: It's pretty ridiculous, isn't it? [laughter] In fact, I wouldn't be talking about any of this if you weren't here asking about it.

There have always been these mystical teachings talking about that which cannot be known, and cannot be "spoken of." Lao Tzu, thousands of years ago, started the *Tao Te Ching* with the line,

The Tao that can be named is not the true Tao.

- these were his first words: The Tao that can be named is not the true Tao!

Q: A good disclaimer!

Wayne: But he didn't stop there! He did not stop there, because the teaching is drawn forth by the people who come.

Genuine mystics do not go out into the market-place to sell their ideas, because their ideas are worthless. They *know* their ideas are worthless. As soon as they name it, that's not it. They *know* they are not purveying truths. That's the currency of the priests and the rabbis and the scholars, *they've* got the truths. They go out and set up churches and universities and temples to purvey these so-called truths. Traditionally, the mystic has not had such structures because he has nothing to sell! So you're absolutely right in concluding that all of these utterances are silly and ridiculous. Yet here we sit together and these utterances happen as pointers to that which exists just beyond the reach of the knowable.

A HIGHER STATE

Q: Are you saying that there is something transcendent beyond the "me"?

Wayne: I am and I'm not. Simply, what we call transcendence is the dissolution of that which is concerned with going in and out of involvement. When that which moves in and out of involvement is dissolved, then the concern, the whole question, everything, is dissolved with it. There isn't, then, some higher state. The higher state is only in reference to a lower state. When you get rid of the higher/

lower modality and you're talking about this Transcendence, there's nothing. There's nothing experiential about it.

RELATIVITY

Q: Could you say that someone like Ramana Maharshi, being in an absolute state, is not troubled with relativity?

Wayne: Are you talking about the body-mind apparatus named Ramana Maharshi transcending all relative considerations?

Q: Yes, isn't there awareness of the fact of the Consciousness that he truly is?

Wayne: There is no awareness of that fact. Such awareness is relative. There is no relative awareness of that fact, because there is no separation in the organism named Ramana Maharshi. For Ramana, the whole question dissolved. The notions of separation and unity were no more. However, because he was a body-mind apparatus who used language, he'd talk in terms of presence and absence.

Ultimately there can be no knowledge of Presence, because there is no-one separate to know Presence. There simply *is* Presence. That's why the negative way of talking about it is often more useful. It points you away from the idea that the Enlightened being has gotten something special; that he's attained something, with the attendant implication that if you're clever enough and industrious enough, you'll acquire it as well. That's why we often speak about Enlightenment as the *absence* of the FSA.

~~~

Q: What is the witness?

Wayne: The term "witness" is one that is used by different teachers in different ways, and different teachings use it to describe different things. There is no universal agreement as to what the witness is.

Q: So what do you call this awareness of everything being One?

Wayne: At the point at which you have an experience of that awareness, I call it "spiritual experience." There is a spiritual experience of everything being One, a spiritual knowing. It is powerful when it comes, and it is quite seductive when it comes. These are the "free samples" Ramesh talks about. With my background, I think of them as the drug dealer's first free taste. [laughter]

Q: And what moved you from free samples to full-on, constant, consistent unity with Consciousness, if I can call it that?

Wayne: What moved me was what moves everything. The event we call Enlightenment is simply another event out of the billions of events in the manifest universe. It is inherently of no more significance than any other event, except to seekers. For seekers this is THE event. There are frequently lots of questions about it and a thirst for books, tapes and discussions such as these. From the standpoint of the sage, it is understood to be simply another one of billions of events.

Q: But after Enlightenment, a sip of water is just as significant as enlightenment?

Wayne: A sip of water is a sip of water. Significance is attached afterwards by the human being and it is relative, rather than Absolute. A sip of water, when you're dying of thirst, is the most mystical of experiences; there is nothing more blissful, more important, more significant than the touch of water to your tongue if you're about to die of thirst. On an ordinary day, that same sip of water is of no particular significance. Significance is always relative and contextual; nothing has any *inherent* significance, including Enlightenment.

EXPERIENCE OF THE SAGE

Q: So, tell me about your experience of "you."

Wayne: Of me? It depends on what this "me" is that you are referring to. If you're asking about the experience of Wayne Liquorman—the name and form and story associated with this organism—that is a very human experience. There is a full range of passion, pleasure, pain and disappointment. But, there is an absence of what is normally imagined as part of that experience—and I stress that it is an *absence* rather than another presence, such as the presence of the experience of unity—and this is the absence of the identification as an authoring entity that is typically there. We can talk about this organism and what's here; all the human stuff's here. What presumably makes this organism sufficiently interesting so that people come here from around the world is that there is this absence.

Q: Right. I'm familiar with that absence, from moments and flashes of that in my own life.

Wayne: What you're aware of is the presence of absence. It must be so. You're aware that there is involvement. Then, there's a moment when the involvement stops, which is the *absence* of involvement. When the involvement returns, you can say there was *absence*, because it is then quantified as some *thing*. The state of the sage is the point where that which is involved, the FSA, dies. It's totally gone. It cannot resurrect. There is Presence, there is What Is. But there is no point at which that can be quantified as some "thing" and experienced as some "thing." For the sage, there is no endpoint to it. There's no separation from it.

During the process of seeking, you have moments of insight when you experience an "absence." But when we look more deeply into it, you actually ex-

perience the presence-of-an-absence that is the result of the coming and going of involvement. That
is the only *thing* that can be experienced. The assumption then becomes that this, the awareness of
an absence, is the sage's state, all the time. But it's
not, because an experience is a presence. What we're
pointing to, for a sage, is purely an absence. So, we
can say that the sage *is* That. The sage does not *experience* That.

Q: So what's it like to be That?

Wayne: For whom?

Q: For the dude sitting in the chair.

Wayne: The dude sitting in the chair, as we said before, is an instrument, just like you. Some days life is
good, some days life is bad. What we're always pointing to in this Living Teaching is Transcendence.
Inevitably, seekers think of Transcendence in personal terms and ask, "The Transcendence happened
through the organism, so what is it like?"

The analogy I use is that you've walked around
today without a stone in your shoe. What has your
experience been of the absence of the stone? What's
it like to walk around without a stone in your shoe?
You will realize there wasn't any experience of the
absence of the stone; there simply was the absence
of the stone. Now if you walk into a room full of
people, all of whom have stones in their shoes, and
somebody says, "Hey, he doesn't have a stone in his
shoe," everyone is going to want to know what it's

like for you.

~~~

Q: If you were to talk to another enlightened person would you both have the same perception of the state you're in? Or is it different for each sage?

Wayne: You're once again thinking in terms of enlightened meat—this piece of enlightened meat named Wayne, meets that piece of enlightened meat, and then you compare the meat. Are the qualities of this hunk of meat similar to the qualities of that hunk of meat? This is meat, [pointing at his body], that's meat and that's meat [pointing at the audience]. There is no enlightened meat. Enlightenment, as I talk about it, is transcendent of the meat.

Q: Well, does it come differently through your body-mind mechanism than someone else's mechanism?

Wayne: The *teaching* comes through differently.

Q: How about the Understanding or the Realization?

Wayne: The Realization is not *of* something; that's where the words are confusing. We, as teachers, talk about Enlightenment as Ultimate Understanding, or Realization, or Awakening. You then have the sense that something has been realized, or something has been understood. It is natural that the image forms that the sage has gotten something: he *got* realization, he *got* understanding. That's the way the language brings forth imagery. There is really no way around it.

The sage has not *gotten* something in Enlightenment; the sage has *lost* something. It gets tricky because what the sage lost had no substance in the first place. Even saying that he lost it, gives it more substance than it's due, but we say that in order to communicate.

Q: Right. But it does seem like something.

Wayne: That "something" is a false involvement, a false perception. When a false shroud falls, what is behind it has always been there. Nothing has changed; it's always been there. This false sense, this misperception, is now gone.

Q: Can you see that? How do you perceive that?

Wayne: No. You don't perceive the absence of something.

Q: You talk about Enlightenment as being the absence of something, and the experience of Enlightenment you've compared to not having a stone in your shoe. Yet, somehow, it happened in your life. And you seem to be confident that that happened. How do you know something that has no feature has happened?

Wayne: Once again we run up against the limitation of language. The event we call Enlightenment happens. There is an event; there is a moment in the history of the organism when that happens. It's something that is self-evident. It is not subject to debate, discussion, or questioning. It simply is. There is no inherent significance to it. The significance is only from the standpoint of the seeker. And for the sage, the seeking is no longer there; therefore, from the "standpoint" of the sage, there's no relevance; there's no significance.

Q: You say it happened in the past and you can remember it. Is it an event you can pinpoint to the minute?

Wayne: Yes.

Q: The experience of Enlightenment, was that akin to realizing there was no stone in your shoe?

Wayne: That is the pointer I use. What we call the experience of Enlightenment, is the moment when that apparent stone is revealed as not having any substance. It never had any substance. It still doesn't have any substance. It was like a hypnotic suggestion of a stone—it wasn't even a stone. So yes, we can pinpoint that it was at that moment that the hypnotic suggestion of the stone was no longer present.

Q: So shortly after that moment, there's a great awareness of a contrast to the way it used to be?

Wayne: That's why I prefer to get away from the image of removing a physical stone. When you remove a stone, you have a profound experience of relief that the stone is no longer there. However, when the stone is a hypnotic suggestion, and it's removed, what is revealed is that the whole notion of stone-ness, the whole *problem* of the stone, the whole *idea* of the stone, all dissolves. It's a total non-issue. There is not a big relief that a non-existent stone is no longer there. It's just not there! The Understanding is that it was never there. So that previous concern with the stone was also part of the illusion. It all becomes moot in that moment.

Q: Can I stop thinking about this now?

Wayne: I hope so! I doubt that I'm going to be able to paint you a better picture of this absence.

Q: Is there some sense of transcendence from one way of seeing things to this new way of experiencing things—has that moment evolved for you in any way for you? Or is it just—it *is*?

Wayne: Again, you're thinking in terms of a new *awareness*, that a new paradigm has come into place. It is not a replacement of an old, inadequate paradigm with a new, more expansive, working paradigm; it is the dissolution of the paradigm itself. It is that total absence that characterizes Enlightenment.

~~~

Q: Why is insight permanent for the sage and not for me?

Wayne: Insight is a phenomenal condition, opposite to confusion. The sage does *not* have the phenomenal insight the seeker has. Phenomenal insight is only present relative to the involvement, the FSA. It is the movement between the two that produces the experience of insight. When that movement is absent, the whole paradigm collapses, so there is neither insight nor confusion. There is no one to look. There is no place to look. There is What Is.

Q: So when the person who becomes the sage has the insight, he's relieved of the involvement of the "me". At least that part of the sorrow isn't there then.

Wayne: That's correct. It simply *doesn't arise*. It isn't that involvement comes and then is removed by the understanding. It simply has nowhere to arise from. So there simply is the absence of involvement; there isn't the negation of the involvement by the understanding. Involvement simply doesn't arise. Period.

Q: Does that bring about acceptance?

Wayne: That does not *bring about* Acceptance, that *is* the Acceptance, the acceptance of What Is in its Totality. The absence of involvement is Total Acceptance.

FEELING ENLIGHTENED

Q: When you talk to people, can you tell who is enlightened or not?

Wayne: I see when there is involvement, yes.

Q: So, I shouldn't try to lie to you about this then?

Wayne: You're welcome to lie to me. I can't tell you how little I care whether you're enlightened or not! It's a total non-issue to me.

Q: And yet there is this conversation.

Wayne: Yes.

Q: Aren't you here to somehow provide some means or help to me, to experience my truth? When you say you don't care whether I'm enlightened or not, that it doesn't matter, then what's the purpose of these talks?

Wayne: Purpose is something we lay on top of What Is. The exchange is happening. Each of us then creates meaning and purpose around it. Ultimately, the Understanding is that this exchange is part of a vast and infinitely complex functioning. Yesterday, you didn't know I existed; you could not have planned coming here. The universe functioned in such a way that we are having this conversation today; you had the free time; you were able to come today, and when you arrived, I was here. That all happened. But all of it is totally out of our control. Totally. *Totally*.

Q: So you're following your nature in some fashion, and I'm following my nature in some fashion.

Wayne: Yes, certainly. And that nature is inherent in the organism named Wayne and the organism named Paul. We can say that through the different nature of these organisms different things happen.

Take the example of a toaster, which is constructed differently from a washing machine. When electricity flows through a toaster, it browns bread. When the same electricity flows through a washing machine, it washes clothes. You can put the bread in the washing machine—it's the same electricity—but it's not the nature of that apparatus to brown bread. And you're not going to get clean clothes out of the toaster. Yet, it is the same energy flowing through both instruments, without which they are both inert lumps.

The Living Teaching points to That which flows through the apparatus named Wayne and the apparatus named Paul and which animates us both. What is the animating force? There's no question that each of these apparatuses are different. But what is it that is common to them? What is it that animates both of them? That's what we're interested in.

~~~

Q: I have a question about the process of identifying with Totality, because that's confusing to me, in the sense that I hear people say that they identify with trees, they see that they are the tree, and the flower, and the bird, they're all of that. But I don't think that that's how you view yourself, like "There I am, over there in that flower arrangement"?

Wayne: Correct. What you are describing is a common step on the spiritual path; seeing everything as One, and seeing yourself as "that." The folks in Zen say that when you start Zen, the rivers and mountains are rivers and mountains. Then as you become experienced in Zen and begin to get it, really get it, the rivers and mountains are no longer rivers and mountains, it's all Buddha, it's all One, they're no longer rivers and mountains. And, ultimately, when Enlightenment happens, the rivers and mountains become rivers and mountains again.

~~~

Q: I've been gradually weaning off the idea of Enlightenment being special. Yet I get the impression that there is a different experience for the organism after Enlightenment. Is there something better for the organism in being enlightened than not to be?

Wayne: Enlightenment is the end of suffering, and so where there is still suffering one can say to not suffer is better. From the standpoint of the organism through which this Enlightenment has happened, suffering simply no longer arises. The suffering is a product of the "me", and that "me" is absent after Enlightenment. There is still pain. The organism still experiences the full range of physical and emotional pain, and its corresponding physical and emotional pleasures are enjoyed. All of those are of the meat. So we can say that Enlightenment is transcendent of the meat. There is no enlightened meat. There are no enlightened beings. There are only beings through which this Enlightenment is said to have happened.

EXPERIENCE OF ENLIGHTENMENT

Q: Was there any sense before this experience happened that this experience was going to happen?

Wayne: Did I have clues or signs?—so, if you see those signs, you could think you might be nearing this? [laughter]

Q: In any case, did you speak with Ramesh about it? Did he "acknowledge" something of some kind? How did that fit into your relationship with him at that time, or over the years?

Wayne: I didn't need to call him up and say, "Hey, guess what happened?" It wasn't significant. That's the whole point. It was not "Oh, boy! I finally made it into the club with you!" The next time I was in Bombay, we talked about it. It was an event that happened, but it was not significant. I was curious, and my question was practical. I said to him, "If someone asked me, 'Are you enlightened?' I'd have to say, 'No' for the very reason that there is no 'one' who is enlightened." What he said was, "You'd have to say that there is Understanding here," and he pointed to the space in front of us. Not here in the meat; it's not personal. It was a great way to point to the fact that the enlightenment is transcendent of the meat. It was a good pointer away from the personal.

The questions we often get tend to personalize Enlightenment: "What was your experience? What was it like? Were there signs? How do you feel now? What were your reactions?" The curiosity is *personal*: "You're sitting in that chair answering the questions: What's it like? How are you different from *me*?"

I can sit here until I am literally blue in the face and say *we are no different*. I can say over and over that this organism and that organism are essentially the same thing, that we are both aspects of the same Consciousness functioning in accordance with our natures, and the next question will be, "Do you ever get angry?"

ENLIGHTENED CONDUCT

Q: Why is it that when people become enlightened they usually stop drinking, running around and doing all sorts of denial-things?

Wayne: You are describing a misconception that people commonly have about Enlightenment. Those behaviors may or may not stop, because there really is no enlightened behavior. All behavior is a product of the incredibly complex programming of the organism by vast universal forces. The "me" does not *produce* behavior; the "me" *claims* behavior. That is one of the most difficult things to get your head around. The "me" has been claiming responsibility for behavior for so long that it's become ingrained that "I do things because I, of my own volitional power, decide to do them; I am the source of my actions." The fantasy is that once you become an enlightened "me," then you will produce only enlightened action, which is generally considered to be virtuous, kind, loving, generous and beneficial. That's a very, very common model of what Enlightenment is, but it has nothing whatsoever to do with my model. In my model, the sole characteristic of Enlightenment is the absence of involvement by the "me." Behavior of *all kinds* can come about from the organism, in accordance with the nature of that organism. What is absent in Enlightenment is the suffering that comes from the involvement by the FSA.

~~~

Q: Does the sage never lie?

Wayne: In my definition of what a sage is, the sage doesn't do anything. He is not the source, and does not consider himself to be the source of any action, but as a human organism any action could conceivably happen *through* him.

~~~

Q: It's funny that some of that old conditioning about what Enlightenment means still shows up sometimes—that old image of Buddha sitting peacefully and never being bothered, the idea that that's how things should be, and that if Enlightenment occurs, then I'll be peaceful, never emotionally up or down. I know that's false, but I'm not sure what to envisage instead.

Wayne: That image is a pointer, not a literal description. Unfortunately, these pointers are often taken literally whether they're Buddhist stories or Christian ones or Jewish ones. The Sutras, the Bible and the Koran are simply collections of teaching stories that *point* to something—they're not *depictions* of something. So you have an image of Buddha as an unwavering presence, unmoved by externals. What is being pointed to is that the Buddha, as the essential Oneness, is unwavering. But what is seen is Buddha, a man—a God-like man, but a man. So it is this man acting like God that people are trying to emulate, and it's impossible.

SELF-CONSCIOUSNESS

Q: When the mind is intensely involved in an activity, such as sports or passionately writing something, we lose track of our self. Is that period very similar to the permanent state of the sage?

Wayne: There are some parallels, but what you are describing is a state that the organism of the sage can be involved in as well. Single pointed focus is a function of the mind. When the mind is totally absorbed in only one thing, the self-referencing part of the organism is obscured. Make no mistake, the self-referencing, when it happens, is part of the functioning of the organism. I make a very, very subtle but crucial distinction between the self-referencing which is part of the functional me, and the self-referencing which is part of the false sense of authorship.

The self-referencing which is part of the functional me is what makes it possible for the sage to know his own name. It enables the sage to find his way home because he knows there is a me that his house is related to. He knows that it was himself who gave a talk for his disciples and not his cow. The self-referencing which is part of the false sense of authorship and which is absent in the sage is what would claim authorship for the talk and would feel proud if the talk was well received, or guilty if the talk went poorly.

GENUINELY ENLIGHTENED

Q: What do you think about all of the many who profess to be enlightened? Is it so cheap?

Wayne: Frankly, I couldn't care less who claims to be enlightened and who doesn't claim to be enlightened. This is solely the concern of seekers. Is this one enlightened? Is that one not enlightened? Is he a real teacher or is he a phony teacher? Everybody has their own opinions and everybody has their own arguments and experiences to go along with them. It is an endless source of discussion and entertainment within gatherings of seekers. There are even websites that rate teachers as if they were restaurants, and they give them little temples instead of little chef's hats. Everyone gets to have their favorites. Everyone gets to have an opinion.

When I was actively involved in that community of seekers I too was fascinated by the question of who was the real thing and who was a fake. One day Ramesh addressed the question and what he said I thought was pretty good. He pointed out that it was the same Source that creates both the genuine guru and the fake one. Both are manifestations of the same Source. Thus within this dance of life, if a seeker is to be confused and his seeking is to be extended, he may well meet and fall in love with a guru in whom there is still an active FSA. For someone else, the converse may happen.

WHO GETS ENLIGHTENED?

Q: Who receives Enlightenment?

Wayne: What we call Enlightenment is not something that is acquired. Ultimately, there is no "one" to have it. It is profoundly different from what we normally think of as receiving something.

It is a problem inherent in language. Language is representative of the mind's structure. The human organism is an instrument of subject and object relationship, and that is the basis on which it functions. The recipient-and-thing-received model is inescapable, because "you" receive sensory data, "you" receive images of "that;" and so "me" and the "other" is fundamental to the structure of the manifest universe. But the manifest universe is merely an aspect that we point to of something infinitely bigger.

Enlightenment is not what you think but rather the ultimate, unimaginable dissolution into all that *IS*.

SECTION TWO:
SENTIENCE AND TOTALITY

WHO IS STEERING THE BOAT?

Wayne: Have you ever been to Disneyland?

Q: Yes.

Wayne: Did you ever go on the motorboat ride through Storybook Land?

Q: No.

Wayne: I'll tell you about it then. After you stand in line for about two hours, you finally come out on a dock. A boat pulls up, three of you get into the front seat of the boat, and everybody has a captain's wheel with which to steer the boat. The boat starts moving and you can decide where you want to go, and set an intention to get there. The watercourse goes to the right. You turn the wheel to the right so you don't crash into the side, and the boat goes to the right. You turn the wheel to the left, and the boat goes to the left. You're doing a really good job of driving the boat. Life feels as if it is in perfect order.

You come to a fork in the waterway, and you decide you want the boat to go to the right. You turn the wheel to the right, but the boat goes to the left.

This is disturbing. You think, "I was doing so well. I was earnestly driving the boat; I was getting my desired results; everything was going great. Now it's not working. I must have forgotten something essential about boat driving."

However, you're in luck, because you are in Los Angeles and there is a weekly magazine full of ads that all say in essence: "Regain Control of Your Boat. Take our weekend seminar. At the end of the weekend you will once again be in control of your boat and you will be able to make your boat go where you want it to go." You take the seminar and do what the teacher suggests.

Then you go back to the ride and get into the boat. You turn the wheel to the right, and the boat goes to the right. You think, "Yes! Success! I've regained control of my boat." You call all your friends and tell them about the great seminar you took and how effective it was. You then turn the wheel to the left, and the boat goes to the right. And you think, "Damn! I must have forgotten something from the seminar. I must not have done it right." But you're in luck, because they have refresher courses for people just like you who have forgotten how to do it right.

So you take the refresher course. You then get back into the boat, and you turn the wheel to the right and the boat goes to the left. Frustrated you say, "I am sick and tired of all this spiritual crap. I'm not taking any more boat-driving courses! None of them work. I'm finished with it!" But if you're a seeker, the chances are all of your friends are seekers too. Somebody is going to call you up and say, "Listen, there's a new guy in town and he's really good. This guy isn't like the last fourteen boat-driving courses you took. This guy is really, really different. I took his course. I turned my wheel to the right and the boat went to the right. I turned my wheel to the left and the boat went to the left. When I got to the fork in the waterway, I turned my wheel to the right, and the boat went to the right." Something in you stirs, and you say, "You got to the fork in the waterway and when you turned your wheel to the right, the boat went to the right?"

"Yes!"

And you find yourself back in another seminar! You can't resist. You are hooked!

This is what my guru, Ramesh, calls "Divine hypnosis"—and it's really a wonderful term. Despite all the evidence accumulated over years, it doesn't penetrate that *this steering wheel is not connected to anything*. Whenever that is suggested, you say, "Yeah, but I turned my wheel to the right and the boat went to the right. It MUST be connected!" In order to maintain this fiction, you totally ignore, or explain away in a variety of ways, all the times that you turned your wheel to the right and the boat went to the left. The reason this term "Divine hypnosis" is so wonderful is that it's not *self*-hypnosis. It's not that you screwed up, or that you have hypnotized yourself into believing something that isn't true; rather, by calling it Divine hypnosis he points to the fact that this way of seeing is part of What Is, part of the functioning of the Source.

For most people, that hypnosis goes unexamined and unquestioned throughout their life. What we're doing here in this Living Teaching, is shining a light on that hypnosis and encouraging you to take a look and see if this wheel is really connected to anything. And sometimes, through that process, insight into the true state of things comes.

TAKING LIFE PERSONALLY

Q: You said that the sense of intention is an aspect of the false sense of authorship. Then all the other aspects of it, such as worry, fears, etcetera, must be impersonal happenings as well.

Wayne: Intention is usually claimed by the FSA. The pointer of the Living Teaching is that all of the occurrences that happen through the human organism are ultimately impersonal, meaning they are not personally sourced, or personally authored. It is important to understand that there are two aspects of personalization that arise following the occurrence of action.

The first aspect is a *functional* personalization. You relate the occurrence to your physical form saying, "I felt that. I experienced that." There is a functional identification with what happens. Thus, what happens becomes personalized as "my" experience.

The second aspect of personalization is the claim of authorship. The FSA personalizes the action as *its* sourced action. The FSA's personalization and the functional personalization are often indistinguishable.

They become intertwined in such a way that you can't readily see where one starts, and the other stops.

The Ultimate Understanding is that *all* events are impersonal happenings. They are happenings that are part of the functioning of Totality. Every thought, every action, every feeling is part of the functioning of Totality—some are subsequently personalized, and some that are subsequently personalized are then claimed by the FSA.

NO SELF

Q: I want to understand how it is possible that there is no "me." How does Source manifest what apparently is this "me," and what happens when the apparent "me" goes away?

Wayne: Actually, there are many ways of looking at it. The discussions about whether there is a "me" or there is not a "me," reincarnation or no reincarnation, self or no self, God or no God, have gone on for centuries. What we're doing here, hopefully, is pointing *beyond* those relative concepts. Those relative concepts are sometimes useful; I have no problem with any of them. They are all potentially vital pointers to an eternal truth. Whether it's a Buddhist or a Hindu pointer, a Jewish or Christian pointer, or a Muslim or Taoist pointer makes no difference to me. I have no interest in the philosophical divergences, other than to acknowledge that they exist. What I am interested in is looking beyond the philosophical viewpoints, to that which underlies all of them—underlies everything, ultimately.

Q: What is that?

Wayne: It is Everything and Nothing.

Q: Does that mean it's a duality?

Wayne: Within the Everything and Nothing is an *apparent* duality. When you look around you there certainly appears to be a duality. There is the appearance of subject-object relationship. There is a point of perception and something perceived—duality. You can then take this dualistic evidence and look back from what is immediately observable, knowable and experiential to what lies behind it. There *is* something; we know not what. And so, this Living Teaching is pointing back, back to that Essence, back to that Source within which the duality exists.

Q: Is the Source beyond the duality or is it defined by the duality?

Wayne: The Source contains the duality. The dual exists, even if we say it exists as an illusion. What is that Something that manifests as duality? This is what the Living Teaching is pointing to: that which encompasses all that is manifest. What is That which manifests?

The basis of the Living Teaching is Advaita, which means literally "not two." So what is this Advaita pointing to that is not two? It's an interesting term—

"not two"—as opposed to calling it "oneness." Because when you call something oneness, it implies two-ness. Oneness is only meaningful in relation to two-ness. By taking the negative approach and saying it's not two—keep in mind *we're not saying it's one*—the question that arises is, what is that not-two-ness out of which the duality, two-ness, arises?

We give this not-two-ness names: God, Source, Unity, Beloved, Consciousness, Mind. There are a million names for the Unnamable. But it's important to understand that when we name it, we objectify it, it becomes a thing. What we are pointing at with those terms is not a thing, not even a really big thing and not even a big *everything*. But the mind cannot conceive of an Everything that isn't a thing.

Q: Is this conceivable in any way?

Wayne: No, not in the relative sense. It is not knowable by the mind, by the intellect. It is not knowable by the senses. In order to know something, one must be separate from it; in order to perceive something, one must be separate from it. And you are not separate from It.

Q …from the "not-two." Well, that's sinking in.

Wayne: That's what this is about: waves that continuously crash into oblivion leaving everything exactly as it was.

NOTHINGNESS AND EVERYTHINGNESS

Q: Is the void the ultimate realization?

Wayne: It depends on what you mean by "the void."

Q: Do you agree in calling it "freedom and space"?

Wayne: I would agree in calling it anything you like.

Q: Well, when I heard "freedom and space," I thought, ah, that sounds good; at least it's something. But if the void is just void, it sounds awful.

Wayne: Well, I don't want it to be awful. There is absolutely no reason it should be awful for you. So, if calling it the void is awful for you, don't call it the void. Don't think of it as the void; think of it as the fullness—space and freedom and love! But no matter what you think of it as, it still isn't It!

~~~

Q: I don't like the idea of nihilism, it feels sort of empty, you know what I mean? It doesn't feel right. So I feel like there must be some way of thinking that's not nihilistic that makes sense, but I don't know what that is. I don't even really know enough to formulate good questions.

Wayne: I don't think you have to worry too much about whether they're good or not. If a question comes up, please feel free to ask it without any secondary concerns about its quality. [laughter]

This Living Teaching is often accused of being nihilistic because what it is saying is that there is no-*thing* that is essential. On the surface that would seem nihilistic, because there is nothing quantifiable that is the Essence. But, on further investigation, this "nothing" turns out to be *Everything*…a vast potentiality. So, it is nothing, literally, no-thing, because the thingness hasn't manifested. The manifest universe is understood to be an aspect of that which Itself, is not a thing. Therefore, while the Source is said to be no-thing, it is literally everything not yet anything.

Q: Could you wrap my mind around it?

Wayne: Well, it's extremely difficult to wrap your mind around it, because essentially the mind can't conceive of this "no-thing." It always turns Nothing into something. Even an infinite nothing is conceived as an object, a vast, unknowable, impenetrable thing, existing within presumably a bigger context. But the Living Teaching is constantly pointing beyond the thingness, to That which exists without being a thing.

Ultimately, you run up against a wall that is impenetrable by the mind. All the mind can do is throw itself up against the wall until the mind either gets tired, or it breaks. Structurally, that is what we're doing here in this Living Teaching: throwing the mind up against the wall until it surrenders or it collapses into Presence.

DESCRIBING CONSCIOUSNESS

Q: When there is a discussion of what cannot be known—the Absolute—it seems to me in some way, the pointers teachers use are always a little off. They always seem to be pointing to a dualistic thing rather than the unknowable Absolute.

Wayne: Yes, you have described the impossible task of the Living Teaching. The moment that we say anything about "It," then we have objectified "It" as something. The very structure of not only our language, but of the mind itself, is such that it objectifies; that is the only way it can function. Terms like "God" often have strong associations for people, so teachers sometimes use less emotionally charged words such as Consciousness, Source, Vital Force, Absolute; the poetic possibilities are endless. Regardless, any term objectifies "It" as some thing. There is no getting around that, other than silence. Ramana said the highest teaching is in the Silence. But you'll notice... he SAID that!

WHO IS PERMANENTLY BEYOND?

Q: When I was with Ramesh, I had a day of a presence of the absence.

Wayne: When that happens it feels sooo good!

Q: I tried to hold onto it because it was so fleeting.

But I know it happened. One of the other students there called it a "taste."

Wayne: Ramesh sometimes calls it a "free sample."

Q: Yes, so I did have a moment of the presence of the absence. Is there a point in time where you fall into that unbroken state and never fall out of it?

Wayne: We can talk about it that way, but it's very misleading. I'll tell you why. That experience you have had of being "in" it is entirely dependent upon that experience being bracketed by the opposite experience of not being there. So the brackets of not being there enable you to quantify the being there; you can only know being there by its opposite. Without an opposite, there is no experience of being there.

You had an experience of the presence of the absence, but that is not the sage's state. This is crucial to understand. The absence is the state of the sage, but the spiritual experience, which is of the presence of the absence, is only available to seekers. That is the relative, experiential taste that the seeker gets, but it should not be confused with the state of the sage, which is an absence, not a presence.

PRESENCE IS PERSONAL EXPERIENCE

Q: Was the presence you were attracted to and pursued before realization the same presence you have after realization? Or was the elimination of the sense of separateness the only difference?

Wayne: It was a quantum difference, not an "only" difference! It changed everything! Before the final Understanding, there is an experience of presence. After the Realization—which is the absence of the separation—there is only Presence but it is not an *experience* of presence. You can only experience something if you are separate from it. Therefore, the experience of presence no longer has any meaning because there is no separation. There is only Presence.

PROGRAMMED TO SEE

Q: Direct causal relations between one thing and another are pretty arbitrary, aren't they?

Wayne: We talk in terms of cause and effect relationships; we tell stories about things; it's part of the drama of life. There is an interesting book that Ramesh asked me to take a look at called *Visual Intelligence,* by Donald Hoffman. The main message is that the brain creates reality. Specifically, the book made the case that what you see is dependent upon rules in the brain. The brain uses rules that it applies to the patterns that register in the eye. Basically, the patterns have no meaning until the brain interprets those patterns according to its rules. It doesn't memorize each scene and then check that scene against its database because things are constantly changing. It has to evaluate and process according to rules. The book breaks down those rules of vision.

This also applies to the fabrication of our total reality: it is a process of the brain. Brains organize

What Is and human brains organize What Is in human terms, so there is a *human* reality. It's very different from a dog's reality or dolphin's reality, because the sense organs are different in each species. The processing cues inside the brain are different as well. Therefore, the subjective realities are going to be vastly different depending on the structure of the brain.

There is no objective reality independent of perception. As humans, we all assemble a similar reality, a shared reality based on our shared human properties. But if you've ever lived with anybody, you know that two people experiencing the same thing can have different realities, different perceptions of the same event. Yet, because of the generalized structure of the human brain, there are sufficient commonalities for us to communicate. When the brain does not form the "normal" reality, we call such people crazy or autistic, or developmentally delayed. Their brains are processing differently from the "normal" shared reality of society.

~~~

Q: So what are your thoughts on coincidences, meaningful coincidences?

Wayne: Events we link together as coincidences happen and the meaning is supplied afterwards.

Q: By the FSA?

Wayne: No, the FSA's sole function is to *claim*. It is the human brain that gives it meaning.

Q: What if certain coincidences recur?

Wayne: Once again, events we link together and call coincidences happen, and some of them recur. The *significance* is applied *afterwards*.

CAUSE AND EFFECT

Q: Ultimately, once I get through all the grief and the wailing, and trying to make life different than what it is, what I am left with is an even bigger desire to know the Truth. This has pushed me to look at the nature of cause and effect. Has my life, all those things that have not gone according to my best plans, opened me to this search, or was that going to happen anyway?

Wayne: "It's happening anyway" (predetermination) or "it's all the functioning of Totality" (Advaita phi-losophy) or "I'm creating it" (FSA)—are *all* overlays on What Is. This Living Teaching simply points back to the fact that events *happen*.

Q: I've got it. Yes. It's like the reincarnation thing: you can flog it and flog it, but at the end of the day, once you understand that Consciousness is all there is, the reincarnation argument becomes immaterial. That's what I hear you saying. You're saying the same thing now. That's just a whole lot of stuff that's going around in my head. It's a bad habit.

Wayne: I'm not saying it's a bad habit. I'm saying if that's going on in your head, that's part of what's happening too.

Q: Yes. So it's the FSA, creating a story, rather than it just being what it is?

Wayne: No, the FSA does not author the story. The FSA doesn't actually author anything. That's the whole point; FSA means a *false* sense of authorship. The creation of the story about things IS the functioning of the human organism. Being human means that you are organizing this vastness of experience in very human ways. The organization begins broadly, first in human ways, and then, more subtly, in female ways, and in female Australian ways; then in female Australian ways with Marilyn's particular history—you can narrow down how that is organized but it always remains part of an infinitely vast, universal organization.

That you tell stories about things, that you think about things in terms of cause and effect, that you react in the ways you do, are part of your programming. The FSA says, "I shouldn't do that. I shouldn't tell those stories. When I get enlightened I won't do that anymore." The common fantasy of Enlightenment is that all of the human qualities that make up Marilyn will be somehow gone. More precisely, the secret hope is that all the bad Marilyn qualities will be gone, leaving just the qualities Marilyn likes; those will stay and all the rest will be magically removed!

But as George Carlin said, "Just because the monkey is off your back, doesn't mean the circus has left town."

~~~

Q: Did you sense a change in your life after Enlightenment? How are you different now than before?

Wayne: Twenty pounds heavier, better looking, smarter [smiles], less hair, different in a lot of ways. Changes happen as a function of having lived so many years since that day. But ascribing changes to any single event, even a supposedly significant one like Enlightenment, is a problematic one.

Q: Is it that you can't narrow down the chain of cause and effect so very accurately?

Wayne: When you look deeply into it, cause and effect collapses under the weight of all of the preceding causes that each cause has attached to it. Yet we employ cause and effect relationship as a kind of short hand. In order to function, the human brain utilizes practical "causal" conventions. But to understand the essential nature of What Is, those conventions are not adequate. We have to examine those conventions and hopefully begin to realize that they are conventions. Each of us talks and thinks in a kind of code that makes sense of the world by selecting out a few points and giving them "significance." What receives significance is dictated by our personality and our culture. Different cultures emphasize different things. Thus, the story that is told about an event will be very different, depending upon your sex, your culture, and depending upon your age and experience.

Q: So cause and effect, in terms of reality, is no more real than the idea of authorship?

Wayne: Cause and effect is a useful tool within a very limited set of events. If you draw a constricting box around a limited number of events, then, within that narrow, limited context, cause and effect relationship has a practical value. You can point to the light switch and say that flipping the light switch causes the light to go on. This is a potentially useful, practical observation. However, upon investigation, we can see that isn't actually the whole truth. Whether flipping the switch causes the light to go on or not depends on a host of other events—payment of the electric bill, a functioning electrical grid, a bulb that has a working filament, and on and on.

In fact, the value in the simple cause and effect relationship model is only when the events in the box correlate as expected. When they don't work as expected, such simple cause and effect thinking limits your ability to problem-solve. If you flip the switch and the light doesn't go on, you're stuck.

ALL IS CONSCIOUSNESS

Q: All is Consciousness. So, absolutely nothing—no event in our life—can go against the will of Consciousness, right?

Wayne: Yes. By definition, if everything is part of Consciousness, then there is nothing that is not part of Consciousness. When we talk about the "will" of Consciousness, it gets messy because we begin objectifying Consciousness as a thing that is exerting will, and that is a very human-centric notion. Will is a quality that you ascribe to people. Of course, ascribing human properties to the Source is something that people have done for millennia. First, the Source is objectified, meaning it is conceived of as a thing. Then, in order to understand this thing, it is given various human characteristics such as personality, purpose, and intention. In this Living Teaching, we're attempting to point beyond such limited definitions to a direct, intuitive knowing of a Source that is Total.

~~~

Q: Wayne, just humor me with this construct that I'm using. Consciousness pervades everything, and its energy is in everything. In our body-mind organisms also, it is present...

Wayne: I'm going to have to stop you there, as much as I would love to humor you. [laughter] Consciousness is not *in* everything. Consciousness IS everything. There isn't "everything" that Consciousness goes into, you see? There is no separation between everything and Consciousness. That's the whole point. So all the rest of your question that comes after that is based on the notion of Consciousness pervading this or pervading that. It is that fundamental notion of separation that we're pointing *beyond*.

~~~

Q: Wayne, I can see that everything is part of the Whole, but I always see the Whole as being some thing. Is there any way to resolve this?

Wayne: No. The moment you think about "It", it's an "it", but there's no getting around that. We are constrained by the very structure of the mind—as soon as the mind considers something, it objectifies it; it has to. So that is why the mystical understanding I talk about is called transcendent—the Transcendent Understanding is not of the mind.

Q: So if it's not of the mind, what's it of?

Wayne: It's not of anything. It is transcendent.

TRANSCENDENCE

Q: When you use the word "transcendence" do you mean, not phenomenal?

Wayne: Yes, I'm pointing beyond that which is knowable by the human being. The phenomenal is dualistic. Phenomena are dualistic in nature. They are part of the manifest universe. So we're pointing to That which *transcends* the phenomena, That which *animates* the phenomena, That which is the *source* as well as the substance of the phenomena.

~~~

Q: So the seeking is to see through the dualism, to have the Final Understanding, so that that illusion is no longer hindering us?

Wayne: Yes, generally the seeker is seeking something—transcendence, total awareness, omnipotence, or whatever—the seeker is seeking *something*. What happens in Enlightenment is the dissolution of the paradigm, of the seeker and that which is sought. The fact that there is seeking, the fact that there is non-enlightenment, is part of What Is. The sage knows it isn't a lesser part. A hierarchy that elevates Understanding above non-understanding is not there for the sage. Both are known to be part of the same functioning, part of the same Whole. The elevation of Enlightenment to a position of desirability and high status comes from the seeker.

WANTING ABSENCE, SEEKING PRESENCE

Q: How do you let go of yourself; how can you be as you are to the point where you don't pay attention to your self anymore and you only experience Consciousness? That's what I'm looking for.

Wayne: I understand what it is you're looking for, but that's not what this Living Teaching is pointing to.

What you are seeking is what the seeker briefly experiences along the way—moments of not being involved with the self, moments of presence. The experience of presence is dependent upon its coming and going. The coming and the going encapsulate the present eternal moment and transform it into something quantifiable.

The disappearance and return of the involvement creates brackets within the Eternal Now, quantifying bits of it and so making it something that can be experienced. For the sage, there is simply the dissolution of the involvement. For the sage, there is the Presence that's always been, but without a returning "me" to quantify this Presence. There's simply Presence. There's no *experience* of Presence. You only experience something you're *separate* from. The sage is not experiencing Unity in the way the seeker does—the sage *is* the Unity. We *all* are—everything is—that Unity. But what is absent in the sage is that *misconception* which is the experience of separation. So, in the sage the final, total disappearance of the separation is not replaced with something else.

Sometimes I say that what you are seeking is Nothing. The difficulty is that when I say that, it gives the Nothing that is being sought, some conceptual substance. The seeker who is seeking *the* nothing has some idea of what that nothing is, based on his "spiritual experiences"—experiences of having known nothing, having been in that place of nothingness. He says, "I want that all the time." The "me" that wants that all the time is the "me" that is absent when "that" is there. But the experience of nothingness only has meaning when the "me" comes back. The wanting of that state is only in relation to that "me" that has re-turned. When that "me" is dead, absolutely gone, then there is no relationship possible, and no knowledge possible. That is the Nothingness, which the sage *is*, but not something the sage "knows" or experiences.

Having said all that, you perhaps heard and un-derstood all of that, and yet the seeking may very well still be there. You may still have that desire for unity, peace, and connection. The seeking energy is part of the organism. So in the same way that you have a physical, biological craving for food or comfort, or sex, or love, or companionship, or air, you have this biological, physical desire to know It, to experience It.

WHAT IS BEING SOUGHT?

Q: Before realization were you like I am now, attracted to that presence and pursuing it?

Wayne: Absolutely! Once you taste that presence, it's like a drug; you go after it. It's great. So you pursue it in accordance with your nature. If you're a wild man, you pursue it wildly. If you're more restrained, then perhaps you'll pursue it in a more dignified, re-strained fashion. But pursue it you will.

Q: Do you know if that helped or hindered the pro-cess that eventually led to Realization?

Wayne: In my model, all events are part of a matrix. Realization is also part of that matrix. All I can say for certain is that in my case, both the experience of

presence and the seeking for that experience of presence, preceded the event of Realization. But I would
stop far, far short of saying that it either caused it, or
hindered it, except to the extent that every event
within the matrix can be said to be the cause of all the
others.

~~~

Q: There are non-seekers and there are seekers, and
there are sages that are enlightened. Is there a choice
involved in the transition from those various stages?

Wayne: Well, what is your experience with that? Have
you always been a seeker?

Q: As far back as I can remember, yes. But now I don't
think of myself as a seeker any more.

Wayne: I see. Was that a choice that you made? Did
you choose to stop considering yourself a seeker?

Q: No, it happened and it was unexpected. Afterwards, I thought I was still a seeker when I tried to
identify myself again. But I've come to realize I'm not
a seeker anymore.

Wayne: When you say you're not a seeker anymore,
specifically what do you mean by that?

Q: In the experience, there was an awareness of something that I could not describe or could ever have
predicted. Trying to explain it afterwards to my

friends was impossible. So it wasn't something I could grasp with my logical mind. As a seeker, I was always trying to use my logic to explain God and my relationship to what God is. In the experience, the gap disappeared. And I didn't know that until later. I only experienced it. So now it's just a sense of wanting to deepen, not define it. Much of what I read seems like an attempt to find it, but reading the words of Ramana, and now reading these books here, it seems very comfortable. I think I'm not positively trying to acquire something; rather, it comes to me. It's not like a traditional learning process. That's why I don't think of it as seeking. A seeker would be a student sitting in class, gathering information. I don't feel that anymore.

Wayne: I understand. It's a matter of definitions. The way you're using the term seeker and the way I would use the term seeker are slightly different. The seeking that you describe as having fallen away is a single-pointed seeking. And I experienced something very similar in my process as well.

The seeking began for me with seeking something—seeking God, seeking knowledge, seeking truth—as a one-pointed effort. It was very strongly directed at "It." Then there was a moment when the seeking changed from a seeking for *some thing* to a seeking that was expanding to include *everything*. It could be called "seeking without an object." There is a sense of opening, of bringing more and more in, without there being any objective one is trying to reach.

This is a very profound shift in the nature of the seeking. In my lexicon, they're both seeking. One is seeking for some thing, and the other is an expansion of the seeking to include everything. But when you say there is a sense of wanting a deepening, of looking to expand that into something greater, that desire is still a seeking energy; it is seeking expansion, seeking more presence or openness. What you described is a profound shift in the structure of the seeking. It is one that is very consistent with what happens in this Living Teaching. The single-pointed seeker is not interested in the Living Teaching that is here. It is only when that shift has occurred, and the seeking is expanding in the way you described, that this Living Teaching has an impact. As soon as the seeking begins to refocus on something specific, this Teaching is here to spread it back out again. As soon as the mind focuses and says, "This is It!"—the Living Teaching is here to re-expand the boundaries.

So, when you say that this Living Teaching feels right, it is because the nature of your seeking has shifted to where this is appropriate. These are the tools that are now appropriate for your expansive seeking energy.

GRACE

Q: Would you call it grace when you start to embody these teachings and life appears to get much easier, full of joy and no suffering?

Wayne: Yes, I like the word grace.

Q: But the path is also grace. Whatever we've done, whatever spiritual practices we've pursued, whenever it starts getting easier, is it only through grace?

Wayne: My favorite dictionary definition of grace is "unmerited favor from God." It's a really beautiful definition. "Unmerited" means you didn't earn it; you don't deserve it. "Favor" points to the fact that you only call things that you think are good "grace."

Q: So that means also that the diseases and everything else you get is unmerited favor from God.

Wayne: If you feel that it's favor, if you feel it's a good thing that you have the disease, then you would call it grace. If you feel it's a bad thing that you have the disease, then you call it "God's will." Unmerited *disfavor* from God is what we call God's will. They are terms we use to describe different things. That which we feel is positive for us is what we call grace.

The most important aspect of this is that it is an acknowledgement that we didn't create it, we didn't earn it, we didn't deserve it—it simply happened. It's a part of the functioning of Totality that we like. This other term, "God's will," is an acknowledgement that the ill that befell us was not our fault; we didn't bring it on ourselves through some failing. It was simply part of the functioning of Totality that we don't like.

SPIRITUAL EXPERIENCES

Q: As I'm sitting here in this room, I'm feeling a lot of energy moving in my body and up out the top of my head. I can let myself fall further into that—supposing I have that choice—or I can come out of that and have more of a discussion.

Wayne: That's right. Either one of those things can happen.

Q: So, you feel no particular greater value in one or the other?

Wayne: What I hear you describing is that the mind is projecting two future possibilities: you can go further into this energy movement, or you can pursue our discussion. You want to know which one has greater value so you will know which one you *should* follow. Then the same mental process continues until eventually one or the other choice is made. However, whether the choice that gets made actualizes as you decide, is clearly out of your control. You may decide you're going to go inside yourself and follow the energy and enjoy it. Then I start talking and asking you questions, and all of a sudden your intellect is stimulated, totally short-circuiting the energy-process you had decided to engage in.

Or it could go the other way. You decide to go inside yourself and the universe cooperates. There are no distracting questions thrown at you, the room stays quiet, there are no phone calls or sirens, and you have a wonderful experience. You will probably say that the reason you had that wonderful experience is because you decided to go inward. The experience reinforces the notion that your decisions bring forth a result. However, this ignores the times that you decided to go inwards and it didn't happen. That's what Ramesh calls "the Divine hypnosis": you focus on those occasions when the results are in accordance with the decision and ignore, or explain away those that aren't.

The term "Divine hypnosis" is wonderful because it suggests that this hypnosis is not your doing. The alternative is that despite the evidence, you're too stupid to see what's going on—so it's really a kindness to be told it's a Divine hypnosis. The pointer is that you're not ignorant or blind, but rather, Divinely hypnotized. Divine hypnosis is the inability to actually see in the moment what you can see later. When the Divine hypnosis is lifted, you can clearly see there's not a direct causal link between the result and the intention.

Q: But there's enough of a causal link to keep you hooked on that.

Wayne: That's exactly what I'm saying. You isolate those circumstances where you make a decision and the desired result follows. You point to that and say, "See, there's the evidence." As long as you ignore all the contrary evidence, you have a whole pile of evidence to support the claim of the FSA.

~~~

Q: I had an unusual experience about four years ago. Something opened up and I was able to feel space for the first time, I felt a presence that I knew was not me. It lasted for about six days, and I'd wake up every morning, having had no dreams, and I felt like a pain, but not a bad one, more like an incredible sensitivity in my heart, and I felt I was like in a cloud, in a dream. Things slowed down…I thought that's it, I've reached it! But then it went away, and then I suffered even more, because something in me woke up, but later it felt like I was acting, it wasn't spontaneous any more. Was that a valid experience or was it a hallucination?

Wayne: What you describe is what I call a spiritual experience, and most people who have had it agree that it's the best of human experiences. Often that is the point at which the sage Ramana Maharshi said, your head goes into the tiger's mouth, the jaws close, and there is no escape, you're a seeker! There's no way out, because you've tasted it, and you'll never, ever forget that; it *has* you.

Such experiences may last a minute or an hour, a week, or in some cases for months. Since it is *experiential* in nature, it contains within it the seed of its opposite. Where there is an experience of unity, within it there is the seed of the experience of separation, and so it will inevitably change. The common spiritual fantasy is that if I get enlightened I will feel this unity forever. The power of that fantasy is staggering, and so is what people are led to do under the influence of that notion. Part of the drama of life is that there are unscrupulous people in the world who will capitalize on the power of that fantasy, extracting all kinds of things from people by promising them they'll eventually get everlasting bliss.

MANIFESTATION

Q: Is manifestation only a partial expression of the Infinite Potential? In other words, is this universe, this life and all of this physical manifestation, that Infinite Potential made manifest? Is it always in a state of becoming and then dissolving?

Wayne: I prefer the notion that the movement from the Unmanifest to the manifest is a movement in which everything that ever was, or will be, arises at once. All relative experience is determined by the nature of the experiencer. The structure of the mechanism through which perception happens will determine the nature of the experience. A dog experiences the world far differently than does a human.

Q: So the experiencer is the essential element in the question of the manifestation?

Wayne: It is what dictates the *nature* of the manifestation, yes. The physicist will tell you that whether something is a particle or a wave is determined by what is measuring it.

~~~

Q: I still don't completely understand; Ramesh said the only real thing is the impersonal awareness of being, and everything else is a concept.

Wayne: Yes.

Q: Expand on that, please.

Wayne: Simply put, Consciousness is the only reality and it is manifest as this universe, which is conceptual in nature. It is perceived through sentient organisms, not necessarily human, but some kind of sentient structure. Perception is a registration that we can call a concept, meaning it has no independent nature. The manifest universe does not have any independent structure. This is also what many theoretical physicists have come to, saying that what something is, is dictated by what is measuring it. And the ultimate measurement tool is the perceiving organism itself. The nature of that organism will dictate the nature of what is manifest. Therefore, there is no independent reality in the manifest universe. The only real "thing" is not a thing; it is that impersonal Consciousness, which is everything.

Q: And how do you know it's real?

Wayne: What we're pointing to is before knowing, before "you"—the pointer is back to the very Source of *everything*. Even the "you" that wants to know how I know that it's real, is understood to be an infinitesimally minute aspect of that Whole.

~~~

Q: Why did Source manifest itself as me?

Wayne: Whenever you ask a "why" question related to the action of the Source, you are, by the very nature of the question, objectifying the Source—I am not being critical, it is what the mind does. But Source is not a thing, much less a thing with a rationale. Rationales are human creations, adult human creations. Little children don't have them and animals don't have them. If you say to a hummingbird, "Why did you build that nest? Why did you build it that way, why didn't you build it over there?" the questions have no meaning from the perspective of the bird. The bird simply did what it did in accordance with its nature. So long as we perceive Source as an entity of some kind, however amorphous, with adult, human qualities, then we ascribe intentionality and objectivity to it. We say, "It must have created the world for a reason," "It must have done this in order to get that." But for our purposes, in this Living Teaching we have to expand the definition of the Source far beyond such a limited, objective definition. Once it is expanded, then questions such as "why?" have no single answer, they have multiple answers. You then have Jewish answers, Christian answers, Muslim answers, Taoist answers and Buddhist answers. You have multiple answers about why the manifestation came into being in the first place, why it looks the way it does, and why there's evil. All of those questions about why God does what God does are what religions are all about.

Q: Are you saying that it's nonsensical to ask those kinds of questions?

Wayne: No, I'm saying that when the understanding deepens, the question itself dissolves. When the understanding is limited to the relative notion of Source or God as a creative object, then those questions have relevance and then there are thousands of answers. There's no shortage of answers to the question! You need only pick one you like.

~~~

Q: Tell me what you think of this statement: "Consciousness, pure Consciousness, manifested Itself as me so that it could experience Itself in this particular manifestation."

Wayne: New Age religions and modern spiritualities often say exactly that: the reason Source manifested was to experience Itself. It borrowed this concept from Hinduism, which says that the manifestation (*Lila*) is God dancing. I have no objection to such answers. I'm not going to debate anybody on those answers. If that is a satisfactory answer for you then by all means enjoy it! But what we're doing in this Living Teaching is looking beyond the notion of Consciousness or Source as a *thing*, with human characteristics and desires.

Q: Nothing can affect It or cause It in any way?

Wayne: The universe is uncaused. There is a beautiful quote by Ramesh. He said, "The universe is uncaused, like a net of jewels in which each [meaning each jewel] is only the reflection of all the others, in a fantastic, interrelated harmony, without end."

SECTION THREE: SPIRITUAL PRACTICES

MEDITATION

Q: Recently I was in India where I met a yogi by the Ganges. He only spoke about discipline and how many hours one must meditate to reach *Samadhi*. I find myself much more interested in how to be attentive and conscious in the moment, and about the fact that there is only one Consciousness. Could this be a trap of mind to escape discipline like the yogi said?

Wayne: The mind that you're talking about that would do something to escape discipline is ultimately a false claimer. You have to look and see if what is *happening*—these actions "to escape discipline"—are the product of the mind. Or is your avoidance of the discipline and your interest in the non-dual Essence a product of forces outside of the mind's control? That's the question raised by this Living Teaching. I'm afraid the Living Teaching does not provide you with an answer. It simply asks the same question over and over. We will see if you have the self-discipline to pursue it!

~~~

Q: From your perspective, having lived this teaching, there's no particular purpose in the evolutionary struggle of being on the path. Is that right?

Wayne: Purpose is always laid on top of what happens.

Q: We make a commentary about what is happening?

Wayne: Yes.

BEING STILL

Q: Last weekend I was at a retreat center, a place where I can go to read and sit alone. There's a plaque there, and somebody mentioned that it was about thought, how just the arising of the thought immediately frames things, like me, my devils and my angels. The plaque there says, "Be still." I have come to see that "be still" means that if the thought does arise, just see it, be aware of it, don't get involved.

Wayne: Blaise Pascal said, "I have discovered that all human evil comes from this: man's inability to sit still in a room."

If you *can* sit still and avoid getting involved, you might take that as an opportunity to look into the curious fact that at other times, despite your best efforts, you *do* get involved. Why is that?

BE EARNEST, BE SINCERE

Q: Nisargadatta Maharaj talks about earnestness but I'm not sure what he means. I realize "I" can't will myself into becoming earnest, so where does the earnestness come from?

Wayne: The earnestness comes from the same Source as any other reaction or action.

Q: What is earnestness?

Wayne: Earnestness is a word that was quite extensively used in the book *I Am That*. I don't know what the word is in Marathi, but I'm told it's a good translation. The difficulty many people encounter is that Nisargadatta Maharaj says that everything is Consciousness and Consciousness is doing everything. Yet in the next breath, he says that you have to be earnest. He insists that earnestness is required for the realization to happen.

Ramesh tells the story of how he went to Maharaj and sat with him. Maharaj said over and over and over again, "Consciousness does everything. You do nothing. You are an instrument through which Consciousness functions. All there is, is Consciousness. That is what you are. So anything that is done is Consciousness doing it." In the next breath, Maharaj said, "You must be earnest in order to realize the Self." Ramesh said he went home and tore out his hair in frustration trying to reconcile these two statements. This wasn't an aberration either; Maharaj did this all the time.

Ramesh said that the way he finally reconciled this for himself was with the understanding that what Maharaj was saying was descriptive not prescriptive. What the FSA heard is, "I (as the FSA) must be earnest." In Maharaj's lexicon, the FSA has no power to be earnest; the FSA is a figment, it doesn't exist as an authoring source. Therefore, he's describing what must happen, so he is saying it in the same way that he might say, "The sun must rise for the day to begin." Earnestness is necessary, but there is no separate individual to author earnestness.

LETTING GO

Q: There's no satisfaction in letting go, is there?

Wayne: On the contrary, on the contrary! The FSA is infinitely capable of claiming even the letting-go, and saying, "I let go so well!", "I really nailed it that time!", "I have such insight and I let go so completely, and the peace that flooded in was clearly a result of my incredible insight and letting-go." [laughter]

Q: So if you let go, all you have is an FSA that has let go?

Wayne: No, the point is that the FSA doesn't do anything!! Letting go *happens* or it doesn't. And then the FSA swoops in and claims what happens. Take a look for yourself; test what I'm pointing at against your own experience.

SPIRITUAL PRACTICES

Q: My focus has been mostly Zen meditation, but I am reading teachers who are saying that practice is what actually keeps Enlightenment at a distance.

Wayne: I'm familiar with that pointer but I'm not enamored with it. Any practice—be it Zen practice or inquiry practice—happens as part of the functioning of Totality. Of course the FSA may well *claim* that happening and become inflated by it: "I'm a Zen student. I can sit twelve hours while people are hitting me with sticks and not flinch. Look at how spiritual I am." That kind of involvement sometimes happens. You can point to that and say, "Look, practice is producing a stronger ego" and in such a case it is indeed an obstacle to greater understanding. But that is a very short-sighted vision. If we expand the scope, we understand that such happenings—the happening of the meditation practice and the happening of the FSA becoming involved—are part of the functioning of Totality. For someone else, the same practice will "lead" to a very deep, humble understanding.

~~~

Q: Sometimes this inquiry you propose reminds me of when I was a kid. I used to try to lift the chair up that I was sitting on because I felt that should be possible, but I could never do it. So I am glad to hear from you that my frustration is not unusual.

Wayne: Yes, it's interesting what these various activities and processes bring about. You may attempt to lift yourself off the ground by pulling on the underside of your chair—and if you do that diligently every day for a couple of hours, and really put your heart and soul into it, over the course of a couple of years, something's going to happen as a result of all that activity. You'll likely develop some muscles that you didn't have before. So, it's not necessarily going to bring about what you're attempting to bring about, but it will bring about *something*. Many of these techniques that are described in non-dual teachings such as Sufism, Zen, and Advaita, bring about unexpected results. They may not bring about the result that you desire, but that doesn't negate their value.

~~~

Q: I heard that in one of your Talks you gave some credit to creative visualizations. Is that true or was someone just imagining that?

Wayne: I am neither giving creative visualization credit, nor am I suggesting not doing it. What I am saying is that visualizations *happen,* and that people are attracted to visualizing, and sometimes that which they visualize comes to pass. *They,* then, draw the link between the visualization and it coming to pass. Obviously, *everybody* who visualizes doesn't get what they visualize all the time. This should not be news! [laughter] Even the very best, top quality visualizer doesn't get everything he visualizes. Why is that? That is, to me, a very provocative question. How is it that some things you visualize you get, and some you don't? Clearly, the visualization itself is not the sole cause, so we have to look beyond just a single cause. And, once you get away from the notion of a single cause, the Pandora's box is open and you're stuck with the entire universe. [laughter] Once you de-isolate the single cause and realize it is linked to something else, you begin to see that it, in turn, is linked to several other things, and those are linked to several other things, and there is no end—it's all linked into one inseparable Whole!

LIVING IN THE MOMENT

Q: I used to live in the moment by focusing on sense perceptions and trying to stop mental images of past or future. Now it seems that during the mental image production, the "me" is actually less involved than when I was trying to control thought. So, living in the moment has become the exact opposite of what I used to think it was.

Wayne: In this Living Teaching, what we call "living in the moment" is the absence of involvement by this authoring "me"—the FSA. The involvement by the FSA in what is happening in the moment, extends what is happening in the moment horizontally in time, into the past and the future. It is the false claim by the FSA that what is happening is "my" doing. The FSA's false claim extends what is happening in the moment, *out* of the moment.

DOING NOTHING

Q: I am still confused by teachers who say that I do nothing. I seem to be doing so many things.

Wayne: Here is where the term "authoring" may prove useful as a replacement for "doing." When we say there's nothing you can do, what is ultimately being pointed at is that the *one* who would author something, does not truly exist. This false author, who claims authorship for what has happened, has no functional existence and thus has no power to do anything.

While there is no independent author/doer, there may well be much to be done. You may have a thousand more books to read, talks to attend, or hours to sit in meditation. Or in the next instant, all activity may cease through this organism named Marilyn. There may be a blood clot on its way to your brain as we speak. It could be a millisecond away from hitting, at which point all functioning ceases in Marilyn. We have no way of knowing what will happen in the next instant, but as long as there is life in the organism, there will be doing.

~~~

Q: I find in recent times that most of my resistance patterns have resolved and there is total acceptance of What Is. I have lost all interest in my career, and there is no motivation to work, though there is a great threat to my survival. Is there any suggestion from you that can motivate me to work, which will of course be part of the functioning of the Totality?

Wayne: Get a job! Quit screwing around! [laughter] Actually, my guess is that the universe may provide the motivation for you to work in the form of physical discomfort as you are lifted bodily out of your home and put on the street, along with your possessions, for non-payment. Such discomfort often provides the motivation to work, though not always. You may simply find a cardboard box to inhabit on the street. We'll see what happens. But it is not necessarily true that your spiritual understanding, or this Living Teaching, *caused* this situation.

~~~

Q: In recent times I've observed that I have lost most of my interest in social life. I do not enjoy the company of others, I love solitude very much and at social gatherings I have nothing to say. I used to be very witty and humorous but now, there is a great silence...

Wayne: Which doesn't get you invited back to a lot of parties! [laughter]

Q: Yeah. In the situation there is no embarrassment, but I feel left out.

Wayne: Understandably.

Q: So my sense of growing peace is not disturbed. Is this unusual?

Wayne: I'm sure if you poll other people, some will have had similar experiences. Whether this is a result of a deeper understanding or the result of some other factors, who knows? What you are describing is a change in the nature of the organism. Whenever there is a change there are going to be trade-offs; some things will be lost and others will be gained. So you say there is a deeper peace, there is a deeper content- ment, but there is less social life. That's what's happening. And it all can change again in the next moment. We'll just have to see what happens.

IS THERE NOTHING FOR ME TO DO?

Q: Are you saying that there is nothing that I can do to get "IT?" That Consciousness will decide when I am finally to understand—or never understand?

Wayne: What I am saying is that you need to look for yourself, to see whether any of what you do is sourced by you. Clearly, there are all sorts of things that you do that lead to various results. The question is who or what is the source of this doing?

Q: I am afraid that if I don't do anything, then noth- ing will get done.

Wayne: What the False Sense of Authorship claims is, if "I'm" not doing it, nothing is going to get done and your life will go into the dumpster!

Q: Yes, nothing will ever get done!

Wayne: That is another of the observably false claims of the FSA. Look at your own life. Take the three biggest blessings, the three most extraordinary events that have come in your life up to now, and see if you created them. Most people, when they look at them, report that they realize they didn't even know these things existed prior to their appearance.

Q: They just happened. They're just there.

Wayne: They *happened*. The FSA says, they *just* happened and they're *just* there because the FSA didn't put them there. It minimizes these incredible things that happen. These events are there as part of the rich and complex universe the Source has produced. The FSA reduces them in value if the FSA can't claim a role in producing them.

I assure you, you are not alone in this. As you sit in these Talks you hear it over and over and over and over again, the same phraseology, and the same diminution by the FSA of the work of the Source. If you look deeply, perhaps you will see that if the FSA was the controller it claims to be, the three most extraordinary events in your life would not have happened. Yet the "me" screams, "If I'm not in charge you're going to be screwed!" If you look closely, you can see that if the "me" *were* in charge, you would have been doubly screwed!

Q: I think that the question "Is there something I can do?" refers to the confusion you mentioned earlier where people think acceptance means passivity, and it doesn't. When there's something that we don't like in What Is it doesn't mean we have to let it continue. You have to accept it because it is what is, but it doesn't preclude you from saying you don't like it. There are a lot of things we may not like in the world, or things we're not programmed to do. We may not like something, but we've got to let it go.

Wayne: If you can! It always comes back to simply evaluating what happened, and understanding that what happened is the functioning of Totality—whatever it is. *Whatever* it is!

Q: It's sort of fatalistic in a way.

Wayne: The fatalism is the "me" saying, "If *I'm* not involved, then what is going to happen is worthless, useless." The fatalism is a negation of the future; it is negative evaluation of the future based on the fact that the "me" is not going to be involved in it. That's fatalism: it's going to happen anyway, so why do anything? It's all predestined, it's all laid out; therefore, I may as well not do anything. But that loses sight of the central point, which is your doing or not doing, is not *your* doing. Your doing or not doing is, in fact, a product of the Universal Life Force. What you do or don't do—regardless of your understanding or lack thereof—is all a functioning of Totality.

EFFORT, PRAYER AND PREDESTINATION

Q: If the picture's already painted, why do I try to make things happen?

Wayne: Once again, we come down to the fact that *you do what you do*. Trying to make things happen is part of what is painted into the picture. The results are then known afterwards. You can't predict with certainty what the results are going to be. However, you will, to whatever degree your nature dictates, analyze potential outcomes and attempt to secure for yourself the best one. That's what people do. What the Living Teaching may help to provide, is a sense that the process is unfolding perfectly; the tension, uncertainty and anxiety are a part of the perfection of what's happening. It relieves you of the guilt that you've screwed up when you feel anxious about something. You are relieved of the sense that you're not a good Advaita student or that you have not absorbed the Living Teaching properly because you experience fear. All that talk is commentary afterwards. You do what you do, including the commentary!

Everything that happens is part of the functioning of the Source, and the seeing of that can happen at any moment. It is the point where you take a deep breath and you say, "OK…this is what's happening right now. Whatever is happening, whether it's the anxiety, whether it's the questioning, or the letting go of the result, I've done my best. Now we'll see what happens next."

~~~

Q: How is the practice of prayer reconciled with the notion that everything is predestined, that we're just living out a script that is already written?

Wayne: It's reconciled very easily: prayer is part of that predestined unfolding, so, essentially, you are *moved* to pray. That happening is part of the functioning of Totality.

Q: But some prayers are answered and some aren't.

Wayne: That's right. Prayer is part of the whole. No event can be isolated to be the sole cause of anything else; an individual event is part of the *whole* cause of the next thing. And so if the prayer happens, we can say that it *had* to happen, as a part of the prayer being answered or not.

Q: But if the prayer did not happen, the outcome would still have been whatever it was going to be.

Wayne: No, because the prayer is part of the whole picture. You can't pull the prayer out. If you do, everything is changed, including the possible outcome.

FINDING THE RIGHT FORMULA

Q: What are we going for? Non-judgment?

Wayne: This may be difficult to grasp but we're not "going" for anything. The Living Teaching may result in the understanding that there's no one to go anywhere and nowhere to go.

Q: So, what do you go by—by what's the most fun? How do you set your goals? You wake up every morning and do whatever feels right?

Wayne: Don't you do that already?

Q: That's my trouble.

Wayne: Sometimes you're in trouble, sometimes you're rewarded; sometimes you have positive outcomes from what you do, sometimes you have negative outcomes. Sometimes you have fantastic experiences and life feels rich and full, and sometimes you're in the toilet. Sometimes people are mad at you. Sometimes people make demands on you that you can't fulfill. That's life.

When you get up in the morning, this organism named Reinholdt has a certain nature. Reinholdt's nature is his genetic predisposition combined with his subsequent environmental conditioning. Your nature is influenced by where you were born, how you were educated, what your family life was like, plus a billion other factors including your current hormone balances, stress levels and blood sugar levels. Everything that has happened since you were conceived has contributed to Reinholdt as he is in this moment.

If you look deeply into yourself, you may see that what you truly are is not limited to this particular form and substance, and what you do is not limited to your intentions and goals.

~~~

Q: For a while I was using the technique of inquiring "Who am I?" and trying to use other things to gain understanding. Then I read your book and I realized that I was trying to manipulate my getting something. That's why it wasn't working. Now I often ask myself, "What do I do now?"

Wayne: This Living Teaching points beyond the events you describe. All of those occurrences happened as part of the functioning of Totality. You were led to my book; you responded to it in a certain way in accordance with your nature. All these events coalesced to give you various thoughts. A day before you first heard the Living Teaching, you didn't know it even existed. You couldn't manufacture it; you couldn't make it happen. It came to you—unbidden, out of your control.

The FSA claims that "I" self-inquired. Not only that, but since the self-inquiry didn't yield the desired outcome, the FSA claims "I" self-inquired for my own selfish reasons. So you end up feeling guilty. The Living Teaching reminds you that the self-inquiry happened as part of the functioning of Totality. Furthermore, the self-inquiry stopped happening as part the same functioning.

~~~

Q: Does the Living Teaching believe in affirmative prayer?

Wayne: The Living Teaching doesn't believe or disbelieve in anything, because there is no Living

Teaching doctrine. There is no principle it claims is true. It is a series of pointers that always point you back to find the truth for yourself. All of the statements in the Living Teaching are simply pointers. You are encouraged to question them all, and to test them all.

Q: Self-inquiry, then?

Wayne: I even hesitate to call it self-inquiry. I prefer to talk about it as simple curiosity. By calling it self-inquiry, we've labeled it; you then think you know what it is, and can say, "Okay, I've been there, done that, got the Arunachala t-shirt. Now I'm on to the next thing." It's not self-inquiry in that way. It is a simple curiosity about the nature of What Is.

Q: By accepting What Is?

Wayne: Acceptance of What Is may come. It may not come. It is not about practicing acceptance of What Is.

PERCEIVER AND PERCEIVED

Q: Nisargadatta Maharaj teaches that you are That which was before you were aware of being around, and you are That now, regardless of this body. You will always be That. What is the "That" that he is pointing to?

Wayne: That's what he doesn't tell you! He says, "I am That," but he doesn't tell you what That is. When Maharaj points to "That," and when Ramesh says that everything is Consciousness, the pointer is always to this unknowable Essence.

Q: Ramesh teaches in *The Ultimate Understanding* that there is no perceiver, that there is not the trinity of perceiver-perceiving-object perceived, there is only perceiving. My eyes looking at you is not "I" looking at "you;" it's just looking. Is there no object of perception and the perceiving of it? In other words, before this body was born and became aware of this earth, was the earth here? Does an object exist independent of my perceiving it?

Wayne: There is no object; that's what he's saying. There is no perceiver object and there is no perceived object. Those are simply aspects of a single Source. They only appear as separate. So there is no "world" object that exists independent of Consciousness. Everything is Consciousness. In order for there to be this dualistic appearance, there must be a point of Consciousness that perceives, and a point of Consciousness that is perceived. But they are not separate.

Q: So that's to say that when this body dies, then Consciousness can apparently not perceive the earth. Does that mean there is no earth?

Wayne: There is no earth if there is no perceiver, no point of perception.

Q: Right. When you die and you're taken away, in your perception there's no earth anymore?

Wayne: Who is this "you" that is taken away? You are thinking in terms of an independent perceiver.

Q: But somebody would have to say the earth is still here.

Wayne: If there's a point of perception, then the manifestation would exist.

Q: Is that independent of my perception of it?

Wayne: What are you? When you say, "*My* perception of it," what are you referring to? That is what we get back to.

Q: When I walk down the street, I see feet stepping on the ground, the ground moving by, and I can feel the weight of my body taking steps. Are you saying that all those things are aspects of Consciousness – Consciousness taking the form of steps, of apparent weight, of air going by? So, I can feel those, by virtue of the senses, but they are forms of Consciousness taking the form of the sense of weight, of feeling, of cold?

Wayne: That's right. There are studies that have been done on people who have lost a limb. The researcher can take a probe and stimulate a point on the stump, and what the person will report is that they feel wetness on their finger. There's no finger and there's no wetness, but there is the experience of the finger being wet. Your experience is a product of your brain function. It is the conscious mind that creates reality, creates experience. There is no reality independent of the process.

~~~

Q: Is it possible to have experience without an experiencer?

Wayne: It is not possible to have experience as we normally understand the term without the dualistic some-thing-to-be-experienced and some-thing-else through which that thing is perceived. So the two objects are the essence of the manifest universe: that which experiences, and that which is experienced. That which experiences and that which is experienced is the basic building block of the manifest universe. In this Living Teaching, however, we point beyond the building block and say, that which experiences and that which is experienced are both aspects of the same underlying Unity.

KARMA

Q: What is your take on karma?

Wayne: What do you mean by karma?

Q: The idea that when we are born into this life we bring with us karma, which is inherited from past lives.

Wayne: We certainly do have inheritances from past lives. Your genetics are an inheritance from numerous past lives. The Darwinian principle is that the circumstances of the past lives will affect the future ones. So if in a past life, an organism was stronger, it would be able to dominate and reproduce because of its nature, and thus you, its offspring, will inherit those qualities. You will get the karmic load from those preceding organisms.

What gets confusing is the religious structure around karma. In most religions, it's all about *individuals* and the *individual's* actions and the *individual's* karma. This Living Teaching supports your investigation into the *nature* of the individual. What is the individual? Does the individual exist independent of the whole? These are really fundamental questions. What is the nature of that "me" that would reap the reward or the negative consequences of its actions? If the individual does not exist independent of the whole, then how does this religious karmic notion of an individual "me" acting independently work?

REINCARNATION

Q: What's your view on reincarnation?

Wayne: I don't have a view. My question is, what incarnates in the first place? When we can get to the essence of that which is incarnation itself, then the subsequent considerations take care of themselves.

PRACTICES

Q: I had a call from friends of mine who are always going to different workshops. They've just come back from a two-week retreat where they spent several thousand dollars to sleep on the ground out in the cold, get rained on, get up at 3.45 in the morning, and stay up until 11 o'clock going through all these different games they had to play—all just to gain Enlightenment. Listening to them, I thought, wow, I just get to go and sit with Wayne...

Wayne: You may not be drawn to them, but all of those practices have effects. There are insights that sometimes come through exhaustion and deprivation. Sometimes when one is taken out of one's normal patterns, things happen, revelations come. So there are a variety of methodologies and a variety of things that one can do, and none of them are in any way contrary to this Living Teaching. This Living Teaching embodies the understanding that *everything that happens could not be otherwise,* from the most sublime to the most ridiculous.

RELIGION

Q: Do you have a personal religious philosophy that resonates with you?

Wayne: Not really. In terms of established spiritual traditions Taoism is the most to my taste. The history of Taoism is unique in that a viable religion never developed around it. As a result, its non-dual essence remained intact. And it remains so to this day.

All the rest of them have turned into major corporations. They are concerned with perpetuating themselves, as is any corporate structure. So none of them do much for me, which is not to say that they aren't useful for lots of people. Lots of people find great solace, great comfort and great value in them. I'm just not one of them.

~~~

Q: Why are all these terrible things happening in the world?

Wayne: Whenever you ask, "Why are things as they are?" you are implying that they could be another way or that some sort of decision was made by the Source to make things the way they are. To get answers to these 'why' questions you will have to either go direct to the Source or ask a rabbi or a monk or an imam. They'll tell you exactly why things are as they are. They've got holy books containing this information. So they will read it out to you: "On page thirty-four of our sacred book it tells us *this* is why." The only problem is that they all have different books and there is no agreement among the books. And all are claiming to tell "The Truth."

This Living Teaching is not here to give you another answer claiming to be "The Truth," but rather to point to What Is, and perhaps, in the apperception of What Is, the Truth in its perfect presence/absence is understood.

GURU AND DISCIPLE

Q: Someone said that the guru shows us a reflection of our own true nature.

Wayne: I would interpret that to mean that when there is resonance between the disciple and the guru—two objects—the disciple may experience a glimpse of the Guru (Source). There is an experience of the Presence, which is our true nature. It becomes experiential because of the resonance.

Q: But there is recognition of a sort, they're saying.

Wayne: Yes, and the joy is in the experience of it. What makes it so potent is that resonant connection with this other object we call the guru-object—whether it's a mountain a person or whatever.

Q: It's an experience, not an object at all. It doesn't live in time even.

Wayne: What I'm saying is that the resonance is between two objects. (I'm talking now about the structure). There are two objects, guru and disciple and for whatever cosmic reason, there is a resonance between them. For the disciple, when the resonance is present, the experience of the Guru (Source) arises out of the resonance. Without the resonance, there are just two objects. Lots of people pass by the mountain Arunachala and don't have resonance. So for them, it is just another mountain. But for Ramana Maharshi, there was resonance with the mountain and so for him, the mountain was a guru. Many people go to visit Ramesh and there's no resonance. For them, he is just another nice little Indian man. But for me, Ramesh is the guru because the resonance is present between him and me.

Q: That's grace?

Wayne: We call it grace because it feels so good. It feels so incredibly wonderful. Depending on the nature of the disciple, there is often a heart-opening and a feeling of gratitude for this object we call the guru because it's the only substantive thing the disciple can attach the gratitude to. The Guru, as the Absolute, has no form, has no substance; there's nothing to be grateful to, or for. It is the guru, as an object, that is the focal point for the gratitude, because it is what can be experienced. But the human guru-object, if he's a sage, knows that *he* is not producing the resonance.

Q: Does the guru experience the resonance also?

Wayne: Not directly. He's observing that experience in the disciple, and it's a beautiful thing to see. One can have a deep appreciation when seeing a beautiful flower bloom; it is this same appreciation the sage experiences when seeing that resonance happen in the disciple. But you don't have an appreciation for the bloom because you created it. There's no personalized sense of having been the source of the flower. It's an occurrence, a happening. And in this case, it's very beautiful; the resonance in the disciple is magnificent to behold.

The guru-disciple relationship isn't always beautiful. In fact it can turn quite ugly if there is still a False Sense of Authorship present in the human guru. What the guru sees is that the disciple is looking at him and seeing God, experiencing the Totality. If there's still a FSA present, it says, "She's looking at me and seeing God—*ipso facto*, I must be God." This is the evidence the FSA is constantly looking for. When this happens megalomania arises and in the most extreme cases, the results are tragic.

Q: Does there have to be a resonance with the other object or between two objects for the disciple to be Enlightened?

Wayne: No, it has nothing to do with Enlightenment; it has to do with the experience of the Guru—which is not Enlightenment. Enlightenment is neither experiential nor relative. Enlightenment is Total.

WHICH TEACHINGS? WHOSE CHOICE?

Q: Some teachers say, "Be alert, watch your thoughts, and observe your breathing." In light of this Living Teaching, how are these practices helpful?

Wayne: I would say that if you go through all the world's teachings, you could come up with a list of suggestions that you do just about anything imaginable. Whether they are helpful or not can only be stated in retrospect. When somebody tells you, "This was helpful for me," then you may try it and find it's not helpful for you at all. Or maybe it is helpful for you, and then you tell somebody else, and for him or her it is not helpful. There's no way to predict in a particular case whether a teaching is going to be helpful or not.

Q: So what do you do?

Wayne: You do whatever you like. You do what you think is best, in the moment. As the understanding deepens, you will begin to see you do what the Source leads you to do.

~~~

Q: I was discussing some concepts with a Vedanta swami, and he replied to me as follows, "Your concept of non-authorship and acceptance is very good, but it is effective only for the matured seekers who have already purified their mind through meditation, *japas*, etc. For a gross person, the concept of non-authorship might reduce the feelings of guilt and bring in some peace, but the uncontrollable mind with its agitations will always bother you." Can you comment, please?

Wayne: When we talk about these concepts of non-doership and acceptance, they are not the equivalent of meditation, *japa*, yoga and the rest. These are pointers, not techniques, and the pointers may be beneficial for some and not for others. We can make a hierarchy of seekers, and say certain pointers are only useful or valuable for a higher-level seeker, and that other things are beneficial for lower-level seekers, but who is going to decide that? Probably swamis.

Clearly, different people are drawn to different teachings. I would go so far as to say that the swami is generally right, inasmuch as this Living Teaching is usually only attractive to people who have gone through various kinds of efforts, and who have practiced various meditations, have done the *japas*, have made the various attempts that are prescribed by different teachings. After doing all those practices, a few people become interested in a teaching like this.

~~~

Q: Do you agree with a teacher I heard speak recently, that "most of contemporary Advaita teachings are dualistic and rooted in deep ignorance?"

Wayne: I think a lot of teachers feel that other people's teachings are rooted in deep ignorance. [laughter] There is often an enormous lack of humility in spiritual teachings, meaning that each claims to be the Truth and feels that the other teachings are ignorance.

Ultimately, I don't think that any teaching is defensibly True; all are arbitrary, all are pointers—even mine! It doesn't take a genius to realize that when comparing one not-true pointer to another not-true pointer, you only get varying degrees of not-true!

All teachings are dualistic. They have to be. The moment you open your mouth it is dualistic. There is no non-dualistic teaching, except Silence. And I don't mean the silence which is the absence of speech, I mean true Silence.

WHO IS ASKING THE QUESTIONS?

Q: So why ask any questions?

Wayne: The questions either come or they don't. I'm not suggesting that you go out and find some. Generally, the people who come here have questions—whether they can articulate them or not. They usually have a fundamental, unanswered question as to the nature of What Is.

Q: One of the things both Ramana Maharshi and Nisargadatta Maharaj emphasized was that the self-inquiry be pursued with continuous, deep earnestness in the asking of the question. It's a guiding principle, isn't it?

Wayne: In some cases, it could be a very potent guiding principle. In other cases, people may well lose sight of that principle very quickly. You'll notice they didn't say where you *get* the earnestness. They said you must have it, but they didn't say where you can get it. Did you notice that part?

What they both then went on to say was that Consciousness does everything. Consciousness is doing everything. They were both quite adamant that Consciousness is all. So, yes, you must have earnestness, but whether you get it or not, clearly isn't in your hands.

Q: So it's the inquiry itself that's important?

Wayne: Absolutely. But, even when you come up with an answer and you say, "Aha, I am indeed not the author of my actions, I've concluded by investigation that I do not exist," the Living Teaching says that that knowledge, which you now have, because it's quantified as knowledge, is limited. It has been stripped from the Understanding and is now a representation. As a representation it is ultimately an obstacle, because once you know something, the inquiry is dead; such knowledge is the booby prize. All that qualifies you to do is give *satsang*, write learned treatises and hold forth in online chat rooms about how things truly are.

What we're pointing at in this Living Teaching is something much more deep and profound which is found in the transcendent Awareness that such statements may represent. Though you may have insight, the moment that insight is translated into a fact or a bit of knowledge, you've taken a step away from the insight itself.

Q: Are you saying that we may not be consciously able to get to the Truth, that there is something that we can feel but not think?

Wayne: Exactly. The difference between transcendent Knowing and the articulation of a truth, is the difference between a meal and its description on the menu.

~~~

Q: In one of your books a questioner asked, "So what can we do with all this knowledge?" and you said, "Not a goddamn thing!" Isn't that kind of absurd?

Wayne: It *is* absurd from the standpoint of the individual with a FSA. With the understanding that the seeking and the answers are *all* part of What Is, it's no longer absurd. It is part of the unified Whole. The entire process is understood to be absolutely perfect.

Q: What's the difference between perfect and absurd?

Wayne: Perfectly absurd!

~~~

Q: May I ask about cause and effect? Does it mean that Enlightenment does or doesn't come, whether we talk or don't talk, ask questions or don't ask questions?

Wayne: Exactly. There isn't a direct cause-effect relationship. What we're pointing at, is that the asking or not-asking of the questions, is a movement in Consciousness. It is something that does or doesn't *happen*. The Living Teaching keeps getting subtler and subtler, and finer and finer, in pointing you to the Source of all that happens. Generally, the people who get here have already *tried* a variety of practices and methods. Having tried through effort to wrestle Enlightenment to the ground, there may now be receptivity to this more subtle and fluid approach.

WHO IS RESISTING?

Q: In terms of acquiring the power of God, Ramesh has said he's noticed that when there's the relaxing into the flow, life seems to go better. It's not acquiring the power of God, but it's more getting into the flow. What's that about?

Wayne: Grace.

Q: I can appreciate that it can't be engineered, but it just seems like an incredible coincidence, nonetheless. There's a sense of doership, and there's an observation that problems occur through resisting.

Wayne: Are you in control of the resistance?

Q: That's my experience—I mean philosophically I don't think that, but experientially, it's the opposite. Resisting things produces an absence of flow, and I can conceive of letting that resistance go, and therefore…

Wayne: Well, *do* it! By all means if you can do it, *do* it.

Q: Okay, I take your point, if I can do it…

WHO IS SEEKING?

Q: Why is there all this effort to make sense of life?

Wayne: Trying to make sense of things happens. It's part of what is manifest as this life.

Q: Is it essential, or is it just because that's what is happening?

Wayne: Whether it's essential or not, is only from the standpoint of a result. It is part of What Is. In some circles, it's becoming fashionable to consider seeking to be an obstacle. The premise is that if you're a seeker then you're deluded, and when you have an advanced understanding, you'll see that the seeking limits you from knowing what you truly are. If you continue to consider yourself a seeker, you're an idiot. So you have a group of people who are still gathering together in *satsangs* and retreats who say they aren't seeking anymore!

I don't consider seeking to be either clean or dirty. It's neither a deluded state, nor the most divine thing that you can do. Seeking *happens*. Some human organisms are created to be interested in what we do here; others you could not drag here. Most people, in fact, you couldn't drag here.

~~~

Q: You've been observing seekers for some time now. What would you say motivates a seeker to be a seeker?

Wayne: I don't really view it in terms of motivation. Motivation is the story we tell about the presence of the seeking. Each individual has a story related to his or her life circumstances that says, "This is why I am a seeker." The real answer to all such questions is that it's part of What Is. Simply put, seeking happens!

ENDING THE SEEKING

Q: I have been seeking very assiduously and consistently for about two years now. It started with a book I heard about on television. That led to other books, and to one guru in the Valley, another guru in Hollywood who taught me to meditate, who gave me a mantra, transcendental meditation, and now, I read your book. Your book really screwed me up, because certain things you said could not have spoken to me more, about this false idea that bliss is what we should all try to get to. We're all trying so hard. And you're basically saying to me, "Enough, stop seeking! It's here, you don't have to go to seven hundred more teachers and read eight hundred more books. Here you are!" So I kinda came here today to finish this whole thing, see you in person, and then I can go about my business. [laughter]

Wayne: Well, I hope you get what you are looking for, because what you've just outlined is, of course, another, more subtle, form of seeking—you're seeking the end of seeking; you're seeking a state in which you're content and can now go about your business.

Q: Right, yes. [laughter] That's correct.

Wayne: I certainly hope that you find that. Now, I must tell you that what my book is suggesting is—nothing. My book is *not* suggesting that you finish up your seeking, that it's all here and that you shouldn't run around seeing seven hundred more gurus, but rather, that the seeking, the running around seeing more gurus—or not—is all part of a vast functioning. So, *everything* that is happening, including all of the seeking, including all of the people you've seen so far and those that you may or may not see in the future, is all part of the same process. The essential question is, who or what is directing this process? Is it you, as this organism? That is the point at which transcendent Understanding may happen.

IT'S ALL A DREAM

Q: Aren't we supposed to see that we are a dream?

Wayne: Supposed to? Who told you you were a dream?

Q: Well, we have this perception that we are this personal ego mechanism…

Wayne: But who told you you were a dream? Did you look deeply into yourself and conclude, "I'm a dream, I don't exist!"

Q: Well, I've been told that it's our ego that tells us that we are a body-mind...

Wayne: You're replacing what your parents and your society told you with what a guru or teacher tells you now. Why believe one or the other? None of it is true! Truth is only found by inquiring deeply within, *to find what you are*; not to say, "I'm a dream, I'm nothing, I'm Consciousness, I'm this, I'm that." *Find out* for yourself! That's what this Living Teaching suggests. It isn't another system of philosophical concepts for you to absorb. We are not here to tell you that you don't exist, or that you're a dream, or that you're truly Consciousness. We are here to support you in asking the question, "What am I, what am I truly about?" The truly worthwhile answer doesn't come from me, doesn't come from books, or from any source outside of you. This Living Teaching is only concerned with directing you to seek the answer for yourself.

Q: Aren't the sages the ones who have the answers?

Wayne: No, the sages are the ones who no longer have any questions. What characterizes the sage is the dissolution of the question.

Q: And that not-knowing, or being freed of all these questions, makes the sages feel very good?

Wayne: No, it simply means that the sage no longer has the seeking. But that is not replaced with a perpetual orgasm, a blissful state of ecstasy that is often imagined.

SUBJECT AND OBJECT

Q: I was hoping you could clarify something that I came across in reading one of Ramesh's books. He talks about the concept of duality and that it implies there is a subject, and an object. He says that the two are interdependent and that one would not exist without the other. I was wondering exactly what he meant by that. For example, if "I"—as the subject—perceived a chair, once I leave, the chair doesn't disappear. You're not going to call me up this afternoon and say, "Elliot, get your butt over here. I want to sit down and I want my chair back." I couldn't quite understand what he meant when he says that one creates the other.

Wayne: Ramesh means that in the absence of a point of perception, there is no object. Not that when Elliot is absent there's nothing, but that when there is no point of perception, there is nothing to perceive. They are interrelated arisings. The dualistic manifest universe (the perceived) arises together with the point of perception (the perceiver).

Q: What I was thinking is, for example, there's a nuclear holocaust, we're all wiped out, and five hundred years from now space explorers come and walk through the door and they go, "Oh, look, a chair." Now, when they weren't there and we weren't there, the chair was still there, right?

Wayne: For whom or for what was the chair there?

Q: Isn't that a different question? The chair was there, regardless of whether or not there was anyone to perceive the chair.

Wayne: Well, that is the mystical conundrum: is there anything that exists independent of perception? The physicists are attempting, very, very diligently, to find the nature of what exists. *Something* exists, but what is it? What is its quality? They keep coming up against the fact that what something *is* depends upon how it is perceived. So, it doesn't have any property itself independent of the measuring of it. Essentially, this means that it does not exist independent of perception. This is not a conclusion that is likely to get you a lot of grant money!

The mystics have sometimes used the pointer that everything is an illusion. This notion—that the manifest world is illusory—is one of the most misinterpreted of pointers. What is illusory about the manifest universe is that it *appears* independent; it appears solid, independent of the perceiver. The mystic says that all of this is mind stuff. What something is, depends entirely upon what perceives it.

Q: So, taking that one step further, if perceiver and perceived are one, then subject and object would be one as well, isn't that right? What we call duality, in fact then, would not be duality, in the mystical view.

Wayne: That's right; duality is an aspect of the One, as is everything that is manifest.

Q: As are the perceiver and the perceived an aspect of the One?

Wayne: That is correct.

POINTERS AS TOOLS

Q: What is *lila* and will it ever end?

Wayne: These questions about consciousness, awareness, *lila*, and how they relate to each other, are ultimately academic. I'm not an academic. I'm not interested in philosophical discussions, comparative religion, or principles of different spiritual tracts. There are many places you can go to get those kinds of answers. I am concerned with what you need to know. What is it that deeply affects you? This is not about acquiring knowledge. My value here, if there is any, is not knowledge-based. So, my explaining the Hindu concept of *lila* and my opinion of whether it will or will not end, is in the realm of scholasticism, or spiritual entertainment.

Q: Although I know more ideas won't help, still there is distress, a lack of clarity and peace.

Wayne: Yes. And so these ideas which we call the Living Teaching are being used to remove the other ideas that are causing you distress. Ramana Maharshi said it is like using a thorn to remove another thorn that is embedded in your foot. If you have a thorn embedded in your foot that is causing you distress, and a lack of clarity and peace, you can go to someone who will use another thorn to remove the thorn causing this distress. When the problem thorn is removed, then both thorns are thrown away. In that sense, we then say that the thorn that's used to remove the other thorn has value—is useful—yet, the thorn that is embedded in your foot may be the same type of thorn.

The point is that an idea is inherently neither a problem nor a solution. It is always a matter of context.

~~~

Q: The Buddha said we mistake the finger for the moon.

Wayne: In that saying, the Moon represents the One Reality, but where the metaphor breaks down is that the Moon, the One Reality, cannot be known. All that can be known *is* the finger. And so it's very natural to mistake the finger for what is being pointed at, because that is all you can actually talk about, see, and experience.

Q: A limited, mind-body object cannot possibly experience a Totality that is beyond the scope of its very nature?

Wayne: That's right, because we are not separate from That. You can only experience that which you are separate from. In the same way the eye cannot see itself and the tongue cannot taste itself.

WAITING TO GET IT OVER WITH

Q: I'm just waiting. I understand intellectually, but the bottom hasn't dropped out. There's a desire to have it all done with.

Wayne: Can you tell me what you mean when you say, "have it all done with"?

Q: To lose this . . . well, who is losing? From what I can see of this teaching, Ramesh and Maharaj paint the possibility of a diminishing, or ending of inner dialogue, or chatter, and I'd like to get rid of that. I believe that there's nothing I can do about it except sit and wait. I don't want to anticipate what that is. It's really a problem. I'm going in two different directions. So I figure it wouldn't hurt to sit down and listen. I don't know what you can say about it.

Wayne: I don't know what I can say either!

Q: I'm aware of that. I don't expect anybody to do anything.

Wayne: And yet much is being done, continuously. One often loses track of the fact that the process of life is ongoing. My being here and you being here, my talking and you listening, your interest—all of those things are part of that vast What Is. So while it's true there's nothing that you or I can do as authoring entities, much continues to happen through us.

That's really the good news, because otherwise you're left depressed and dulled out, with the FSA's nihilistic counterclaim that "there is nothing I can do" sapping the life energy. It puts a grey blanket on everything. This Living Teaching points out that there is much to be done. As long as breath exists in the body, there still are many thoughts to be thought, many feelings to be felt, many actions to perform and many experiences to have.

What fuels so much of human suffering is the notion that what is observed as dark and painful and unpleasant shouldn't exist, that somehow, it is a fundamental flaw in the universe that things are as they are. Implicit in that observation is the attitude that I know what is right for the universe and so those conditions need to be corrected. Often the weight of that correction falls on the FSA in the thought that "I" am somehow responsible for all of this. There is a subtle claiming of authorship for it. It's subtle, but it's there. That involvement is what produces the suffering attendant to the pain of life.

As the Living Teaching takes hold, reducing the strength of this FSA, there is often a reduction in suffering. The pain is still there, the misery in the world remains, there is still unhappiness and ugliness. However, the sense that "it should not be as it is" is reduced, and with it, the suffering is reduced. When the suffering is reduced, much of what is beautiful about the world becomes visible. The result is that happiness and unhappiness are seen to be in balance, and beauty and ugliness are seen to be in balance.

Q: Would that also be true of other drives that one might have? I think that this seeking that exists within me has been driven by a fear that I could not name. It's been there since I was a child. There is some kind of existential horror. I think that seeking is like a condition, a bad itch. I don't want to say it's an illness. But it's something like a chronic condition.

Wayne: That existential angst, that quality of unfettered, free-floating fear, unconnected to anything specific, is what I would characterize as the fear inherent to the FSA. It is a fear grounded in the fact that the FSA knows its own powerlessness; it knows that despite its claims of potency it can't control the universe. It can't actually *do* anything. And yet, it's built up an incredible facade of potency, claiming to be able to do whatever it likes.

Q: That's it. And that's depressing. You think you're making progress, but then you realize there's no such thing as progress. When you talk about this, I realize that other people experience some version of this. I'm sixty-five years old. I thought when I was thirty I'd straighten this out in two or three years!

Wayne: What you're saying is known by virtually everyone in the room, and is relevant to everyone. It isn't just your unique problem or your unique situation.

SECTION FOUR: THE LIVING TEACHING

AIM OF THE TEACHING

Q: If everything is as it is and nothing is wrong, then to what degree is the Living Teaching helping anyone?

Wayne: The Living Teaching is simply a collection of tools. The outcome of the application of those tools is varied. There isn't a promise that by applying these tools you'll be helped. I've seen two people sit in the same talk, read the same books, be exposed to the same teaching, and while one person gets a deep, intuitive understanding that brings a real peace to her life, the other gets depressed, gets frustrated, gets nihilistic and dark. Same teaching, same tools; in one case it brings about peace, and in the other it brings misery.

Q: So the understanding of these tools is liberation of sorts, which is the full acceptance?

Wayne: No, it is not the *understanding* of the tools; it is what we'll call the positive *effect* of the tools. It is not the student's grasp of the concepts that brings about success. It is the application of the tools in such a way that there is an epiphany, an intuitive knowing.

Q: But in that intuitive knowing, there is what?

Wayne: There is nothing!—in the most profound sense. There was a book many years ago, by Robert Heinlein, called *Stranger in a Strange Land.* Heinlein used the term "grok" to describe a moment of deep and total understanding, but it was not an understanding of anything. Wei Wu Wei uses the word "apperception" to point to the same thing; this sudden deep intuitive knowing, which is not objective in nature. Apperception means perception without a perceiver or a perceived object. It's a non-dualistic state. Even to use the word "state" is too gross a term, because what it is pointing to is a Totality of identification, transcendent of dualistic understanding.

Q: Is this what others may say is like Pure Being?

Wayne: Enlightenment, Pure Being, Unity with What Is. There are a variety of very beautiful, poetic descriptions of this undescribable "state" which is not a state.

CHANGING MY PROGRAMMING

Q: You say that the programming is built into the mind-body organism. Would one who follows the Living Teaching find himself able to change the programming? If a person was predisposed to anti-social behavior, might that person, through the study of the Living Teaching, use the teaching to reprogram himself so that he would no longer have the predisposition towards anti-social behavior?

Wayne: The effect of exposure to this Living Teaching is variable and limitless. Some people are affected positively, and others negatively. For example, a person comes here and is exposed to the Living Teaching; after this exposure, his programming changes and as a secondary result, his life changes. In one particular case, certain anti-social behaviors may fall away. In another case, these same anti-social behaviors may begin. The point in all this is that it is the *teaching* that can be said to bring about the change in the programming. It is not the individual who authors the change in the programming.

Q: Would that be fair to say that the Living Teaching differs from Buddhist teachings in that those teachings have a formalized objective to end suffering?

Wayne: Whatever the objective of any teaching, the effect of the teaching is not predictable. You need only to look for yourself to see that.

DESTINY AND FREE WILL

Q: I was wondering if you could maybe review the teachings regarding destiny with me?

Wayne: To understand either destiny or free will, we have to first consider the Totality of What Is. Everything that ever was, or ever will be, is part of this vast Totality of What Is. Destiny and free will are simply strategies for making sense of the vastness of What Is. Both terms are a kind of practical shorthand in which the holographic universe is made linear. The linear conception is an overlay. It's an intellectual, organizational overlay on top of the Totality of What Is. Neither destiny nor free will actually describes the functioning of the universe. Yet people subscribing to one overlay endlessly argue with people subscribing to the other overlay. There is, ultimately, neither destiny nor free will. There is only What Is.

Q: I'm programmed to subscribe to one overlay rather than the other?

Wayne: Yes, as a conditioned organism with a brain that works in a limited and linear fashion, you will order the What-Isness *somehow*. You must do this in order to function in the world, because the What-Isness is too vast to absorb without a framework. The framework allows you to pick out a couple of aspects of the What-Isness, and cobble them together into a "reality." If you had to take in the entire What-Isness at once, your brain would overload. There is too much

What-Isness to possibly process by such a finite apparatus as the brain. So the brain imposes a box upon the What-Isness saying, "Within this box, we will make sense of things by linking this event with that event—cause and effect—and relate these various objects, one to the other." That's what we call "knowledge." This framework is our world view. Our world view is, by definition, a human one, because it is created by the limitations of the human brain and the human senses. These define what can be taken into the human box. Within the human box is the question of free will versus destiny.

The collective human experience, comprised of our literature, our science and our philosophy, is an accumulation of the thoughts and investigations assembled by humans over our recorded history. We inevitably have a human-centric perspective, but this human perspective is minuscule in terms of the vastness of What Is. Furthermore, it's not central, even though we like to think of the human perspective as being at the very heart of the manifest universe. But upon even the most cursory investigation, this is a difficult proposition to support. A brief look into astronomy will reveal that this planet is a little speck of dust, in a trivial galaxy, in a backwater of the universe. It's not at the center of things. It's way off to the side!

Q: Well, I like the concept that your programming determines if you will subscribe to free will or destiny. I'm a yoga instructor and the teachers who teach in this tradition mostly have a belief in free will. They believe that you can alter your destiny by spiritual practice. I've had new conditioning in my life, due to this and other non-dual teachings, that has helped me to embrace destiny more.

Wayne: Each tradition has its strengths and weaknesses. The arguments are endless and ongoing. In fact, this particular argument has been going on for millennia. If you find it entertaining to engage in such discussions with people, why not do it? It's fun! But understand that your yoga school's beliefs and this Living Teaching, and whatever else you may read or hear, are not the Truth. It isn't that you now have the true way of describing the universe when you talk about destiny, and that the people who believe in free will or the randomness of events are mistaken. *None* of them is true. They are simply different ways of organizing What Is.

Many people, getting more deeply into the Living Teaching, find that as this way of understanding deepens, it brings more peace. Inevitably, when you rely on yourself to author success in your life, you're always a step behind. Successes may come, but they do not bring a lasting peace. You're always in a state of chasing. The benefit of claiming authorship is that you can measure progress. You can say, "I haven't got it yet—whatever *it* is—but I'm getting better. I'm better than that guy, therefore, I'm a success." But when you lay down to go to sleep at night, and you don't have anybody else around, there is a voice within that whispers, "I'm not making it, I'm not good enough, I'm not as good as that guy, I haven't gotten there yet." It is insidious.

The Peace that comes with the acceptance of everything being perfect, as an aspect of the Whole, is much more subtle, much more elusive. However, it is a Peace that, when it comes, does surpass all understanding.

~~~

Q: So what do you say about free will?

Wayne: I say that if you've got it, use it! You either have free will, or you don't. It's like being pregnant; you're either "it" or you're not. The notion of partial free will is as ludicrous as being partially pregnant. You either have free will, as a conceptual possibility, or you don't, and I'm willing to go along with you on either one. If you say you've got free will, I say, God bless you, exercise it beautifully. Be kind, generous, loving and wonderful to everybody; exercise your free will for the good of mankind, for the good of yourself, for the good of the universe. Start right now. Come back in a week and we can talk again. If you come and you show me you were successful, I will happily prostrate myself at your feet. If you tell me you don't have free will, then I would invite you to investigate what is the source of your actions.

Q: So if there is no free will, then all the crazy, insane, crappy things that go on are supposed to be going on?

Wayne: If that is true, then you are going to have to completely redefine what God or Source is. You've identified crap going on in the world—meaning stuff you don't like, that you don't feel is very productive or beneficial—and you say, "That's *not* Source, that's not godly." Logically, then it must be something else. Once you've set up "godliness" and "something-elseness," you have the basic dualistic model of most of the world's religions.

In this Living Teaching, when we talk about God or Source, there is no other. There is only God, which is Everything. Within that Everything, exist both the stuff you like, and the stuff you don't like, the crap and the beauty, the health and the sickness, the joy and the sorrow, the pain and the pleasure—all of the polaric opposites. They exist within the Whole, and it is then understood that everything is God, everything is Source. Even the jerk cussing at you on the freeway is Source. Admittedly, that's a little more difficult to get your head around. Most people prefer the idea of Source as being puppies and dolphins and rainbows!

Q: So what is the heart of the matter?

Wayne: The heart of the matter is: What is authoring everything? What is the Source? If you tell me it is you, as a body-mind organism exercising your free will, I have no desire to dissuade you from that belief.

Q: So the heart of the matter is, what's authoring it?

Wayne: Yes! What is causing you to pay your bills and somebody else not to? What causes you to exercise restraint on the freeway and causes somebody else not to? What is the source of your blessings and your curses? Is it *you*?

Q: Of course not.

Wayne: OK, that's an important step. If it's not you, then it's something other than this "me" that claims to be the author. When you say, "I am choosing, I'm deciding," that's usually tied to a sense of authorship.

Q: So the mistake is to believe that I will my life, that I have the power to will my life?

Wayne: It's not a mistake; it's simply the mechanism that brings suffering. When the sense of authorship is present, the potential for suffering is present.

~~~

Q: Our actions seem paradoxical in that they are neither the product of free will, nor are they determined in any measurable sense. Is that so?

Wayne: It is paradoxical, because our actions are part of a Whole and yet they are *understood* in relative terms, such as "predetermination" or "free will." There is only one way a paradox can be disposed of. It can never be resolved—because a paradox, by its nature, is not resolvable since it has a logical incongruity within it. It can only be *dissolved* with a greater understanding, by which I mean that it can be encompassed by an overriding understanding that allows for *both* of the mutually exclusive components.

NO CHOICE

Q: So, we don't have any choice?

Wayne: I'm not here to tell you you have a choice or that you don't have a choice. I'm saying that, clearly, choices get made. We're looking at the *source* for the choice that gets made. Is it local or Universal? Is this body-mind apparatus an aspect of the Total? Or is it its own source? Does it source its actions? Does it source its reactions? Those questions are raised here. And only you can answer them for yourself. There is no doctrine. I'm not telling you what you should be-lieve, or what should happen. This Living Teaching is an open invitation for you to look for yourself.

WHO IS TEACHING?

Q: You have regularly scheduled talks on the advaita.org web site. Do you view the schedule as something you "should" do, or "need" to do? What motivates you to sit down and perform this service?

Wayne: What motivates me to sit down here is that which motivates me to eat and to breathe and to sleep. The very same Source, the very same energy is op-erative in my sitting down here and in my breathing. There is no more of a FSA attachment to my sitting down here—in terms of claiming to be the source of this action—than there is to my breathing.

~~~

Q: Your answers, even to the most complex questions, always come so quickly, and yet always seem perfect. If they do not come from you, where do they come from?

Wayne: They come from the same Source that everything comes from. And the awkward, mangled answers also come from the same Source. [laughter]

KNOWLEDGE

Q: Wayne, where does your knowledge come from?

Wayne: The concepts that I articulate come from my experience; they come from my background, my guru, my education. The programming of this organism produces these utterances we call communication. I'm not claiming to speak from a truth, meaning that I claim to know something that cannot be disputed. I have no such knowledge, because any knowledge has to be relative. If it's relative, it can be argued, disagreed with. So, the only Absolute Knowledge or Understanding is that which cannot be spoken, and cannot even be known.

WHO IS SPEAKING?

Q: You, I assume, are connected—and aware of this connection—with Consciousness.

Wayne: You assume incorrectly. There is no aware-ness of a connection because there is no separation. Connection can only exist where there is separation, but there is no separation. So there is the presence of Consciousness, certainly, but there is no separate awareness of that presence of Consciousness.

~~~

Q: Wayne, you said that when you use "I", it is as Wayne, and when Ramesh uses "I", he speaks as Con-sciousness—if I have that right.

Wayne: No I don't think so. Ramesh generally speaks in the first person, as Ramesh. It was Nisargadatta Maharaj who used the technique of speaking from the perspective of Consciousness for his teaching pur-poses. He wasn't speaking from the perspective of Consciousness in his business relationships or family relationships. When he was teaching he used that pointer of talking as if he were Consciousness Unmanifest.

~~~

Q: Would you explain again why using the expres-sion that the sage is aware of his connection with Consciousness is not valid?

Wayne: Because in order for things to be connected, they have to be separate in the first place. In the final Understanding that separation does not exist. There-fore, there is no possibility of connection. There is simply Oneness. That is why I say there is no non-

dual *perspective*. All perspective is by its very structure, dualistic. All experience of connection, all
experience of unity, all experience of oneness is dependent upon separation.

Q: So there really is no Oneness either, because Oneness is built upon the idea of separation.

Wayne: Yes.

Q: It doesn't leave much then.

Wayne: It doesn't leave *anything*. When we talk about
Enlightenment or Oneness it is much ado about Nothing!

ONENESS IS ALL THERE IS

Q: Couldn't what is described as the non-dualistic
state just be what the people who are called sages
made up? Who says that it's for real?

Wayne: It is not real. It's a pointer. It is not real in the
sense that it can be experienced. There is no non-dualistic state. Every state is dualistic by nature. It has
to be.

Q: But this teaching says that Oneness exists beyond
what we are aware of or understand.

Wayne: There is no "beyond." Oneness exists and is
all there is.

Q: How do we know that?

Wayne: These are merely pointers of this Living Teaching and not something to be experientially known. What may happen is what Wei Wu Wei calls "apperception," which is a knowing without a knower. We can also call it mystical knowing.

Q: Well, who said so?

Wayne: I'm saying so. And it is not the truth. It's a pointer, a teaching tool. Mine. *My* tool.

Q: So your Living Teaching is like another religion, in a way, which some believe or many believe?

Wayne: It can certainly be turned into a religion by believers, despite my efforts to the contrary. But in its essence, this Living Teaching is simply a collection of pointers that people are invited to examine and use, rather than believe in.

Q: Yeah. If you believe in something, that's a religion.

Wayne: That's right. Taking something as an *a priori* truth—"it is, because I believe it"—is the basis for most religions. Hopefully, we are not building another religion here, but rather pointing incessantly to What Is. Then, when the mind attempts to build a philosophical or religious structure around this What Is, we will try to kick it down.

Q: But you are convinced that there is the Oneness?

Wayne: No, I am not convinced there is Oneness at all. There is no conviction, there is no belief, there is no truth that I "have" and that I am expounding to you. None! Everything that I say is a *pointer*, not a truth. Hopefully, it will point you to look into yourself to see that there is Existence there. That is the only Truth, and it must be seen, not believed.

WE ARE ALL ONE

Q: Isn't it true that we are all one in Essence? Can't we take that as a doctrine?

Wayne: We can certainly turn it into one! It is a pointer that is used in this Living Teaching, certainly—that everything is One. But it's a concept. It's a tool. It's not the truth.

Q: That's *not* the truth?

Wayne: It's not the truth! The statement, "Everything is One," is an *idea.*

Q: It can anchor one into a feeling of comfort.

Wayne: It may, in some cases, anchor one into feelings of comfort. In others, it may be used as an excuse to do unspeakable acts: "Oh, it's all One. God is doing it. I've got no responsibility. I'm going to kill whomever I want. It's all the Oneness doing it anyway." For one person, the idea is associated with an experience of peace and for another, it is associated with mass murder. In neither case is it true. The Truth, as we're pointing to it, is bigger than an idea.

NO DOER

Q: I've come to a contradiction in the Advaita teaching, in that it says there is no doer. This seems contradictory to the scientific tenet that it's impossible to prove the nonexistence of anything. I can prove something exists, you know, but there is actually no way you can say that something doesn't exist. So how can Advaita teachers say that the doer, or the ego, or the soul doesn't exist?

Wayne: You'll have to ask an Advaita teacher who says that.

Q: You say there is no doer.

Wayne: I do *not* say there is no doer. I absolutely do not say that. What I propose is that you investigate. As soon as you say, "there is a doer," or "there is no doer," "there is no free will," or "there is free will" the whole investigation is dead. You take that factoid that there is no doer, or there is a doer, and you swallow it. Then you have that factoid inside you, but so what? The process is dead. And what this teaching is about, and the reason I call it The Living Teaching, is because it is without tenets, it is without doctrine, and it is without all the philosophical debate that saps the life out of simply following the curiosity that is alive in you. The Living Teaching points you to look for yourself, to find your essential Self, to hopefully have an insight that is deep and profound. That's the only thing that has any true value in a mystical sense. This Living Teaching is neither philosophy nor religion.

~~~

Q: If there is no path, then does it make any difference what I do? Why should I continue to study this Living Teaching if it's not going to lead to Enlightenment?

Wayne: It may well make a difference what you do. The real question is do you author what you do? When the FSA is present, the "What the hell should I *do*?" is a continuous problem. Then the Living Teaching comes along and you begin to glimpse the lie that is implicit in the FSA, concluding that it's stupid to do A if it's not going to produce B. But the problem is we don't *know* what A is going to produce!

All we can really say is that doing *happens.* You have an interest in spirituality that leads you to come here. Then we talk, and then you have clarity or you have further confusion. Each doing is connected to another doing. The story we tell about this chain of doing is cause and effect: A caused B, and then B caused C. Putting aside the discussion of the usefulness of the concept of cause and effect for the moment; we can simply say that the human organism understands things in terms of cause and effect. From that perspective, you might conclude that your effort—

following the Living Teaching for example—is not going to cause what you want it to cause, so why should you do it? The presumption is that you are the author of it. That's where the authorship and the doing get confused.

When you look deeply, you may begin to understand that the "doing" is *happening* as part of the functioning of the universe. You being here is the result of a myriad of forces—you had access to a computer, you were moved to type something into a search engine, my name came up, the server worked and the webpage came up, you read the webpage, it resonated with you—the number of things that had to be in place for you to be here is mind-boggling. We can say that the Source is doing those things. What the Living Teaching points to again and again, is this unified Whole within which everything happens. All of the events within the Whole are understood to be simply *aspects* of the Whole. Everything! No exceptions!

TOOLS FOR LIVING

Wayne: Much of what spiritual seeking is often about, is to find a tool or a technique that one can apply to one's life to solve one's daily problems. This Living Teaching, as I've often said, is not a tool for living. In other words, you can't *apply* this Living Teaching. The direct application of the Teaching to a particular life situation is fairly nonsensical. People sometimes try to do it, but they end up with very mixed results. The Living Teaching itself is a tool for *understanding.* And that understanding, when it comes about, makes living easier, more palatable or more peaceful. But that's a by-product of the understanding.

Q: So there's nothing in this Living Teaching to help you prepare, to help you to open yourself up?

Wayne: This brings us back to the nature of the self that would open itself up. We again come back to that basic question of what is the nature of the self that would prepare, that would act this way or that way if it were in control? *Is* it in control?

Q: I'm remembering that Ramana Maharshi and Nisargadatta, and I think even Ramesh, were posed with the question at some time or another of somebody saying, "Well, here you are talking about all this lovely stuff, yet there is misery out there in there world. So what are you doing about it?" And their answers were very similar, "Whatever I'm doing is enough."

Wayne: That's right. All of us, whether we know it or not are complete unto ourselves in this moment. All our actions are the product of vast universal forces. What we will do in the next moment, we'll have to see. For the sage, there is never the possibility of it being otherwise.

~~~

Q: The teachings of a number of awakened spiritual teachers sound remarkably similar to your teaching, but they speak about the temporary coming-back of identification as part of the dance of What Is, but their true nature is untouched. Does this make sense to you?

Wayne: I have no desire to talk about anybody else's teaching. If it makes sense to you, if you like it, terrific, but understand that *all* these teachings are *pointers*. They are not truths. So, if you like one set of pointers, don't worry that it does not match with another. You can spend the rest of your life trying, but you're not going to discover which one of them is true. Neither of them is true. No teaching is true. They are all *pointers*.

In this Living Teaching, I make a distinction between spiritual experience and the Final Understanding. That's my notional distinction. I make it conceptually very clear that the Final Understanding is total, final, irrevocable, and complete. Nothing is left to come back. That's my concept. The relative states and stages before that are what I would call "spiritual experiences," during which the FSA recedes and then comes back. This type of spiritual experience is sometimes called "awakening." What the seeker is seeking is to be awakened. So when you tell him he's awakened and now he's just stabilizing into his awakening, or his awakening is becoming finalized, or whatever the explanation, it makes him happy. I am all for people being happy but I make the distinction to hopefully eliminate some of the confusion that surrounds the subject of Enlightenment.

POSITIVE AND NEGATIVE PATHS

Q: I've read a lot of Ramana Maharshi. Initially, I thought that what he and Ramesh say would be the same, but they appear to be very different. There seems to be an emphasis on the Self with Ramana Maharshi, as a kind of all-encompassing something-ness, but there's such an emphasis on nothingness with Ramesh. Of course I know that it amounts to the same, but Ramana's approach seems a lot more positive.

Wayne: I'm not sure Ramesh would agree with me, but I would go so far as to say a lot of Ramesh's "negative" approach served as a counterbalance to the "positive" approach of Ramana. When people came to Ramesh after having studied Ramana's teaching, he lifted their burden of believing that Ramana's teachings were an absolute Truth.

The statements that Ramana made, when talking about the Self, the characteristics of the Self, discovering the Self, reuniting with the Self, and all of those "positive" statements, are readily misinterpreted as descriptors of some *thing*. There were many people who had had that kind of indoctrination prior to coming to Ramesh. If the student was to move forward, that false understanding had to be stripped away. One of the ways to strip that away, was to counterbalance it with a *neti-neti*, a not-this and not-that approach.

So curiously, after Ramesh did that for fifteen years or so, he then switched to a positive approach. His latest books are much more about a positive form of self-inquiry, such as to pick one of the events out of your day that you feel was your doing, and to look at it to see whether it was, in fact, your doing—a deconstructing of personal authorship. You should have heard the screams of the people in the talks when he first rolled this out. They were moaning, "How can you say this? How can you tell people to do this after you've been saying that there is nothing to do and no-one to do it for all these years?"

Q: So how did he bridge from one statement to the next?

Wayne: Oh there's no bridge.

Q: It's just a paradox?

Wayne: Absolutely, a paradox, and the paradox is implicit in all these non-dual teachings. "Form is nothingness, nothingness is form." What could be more paradoxical than that? Yet it is a very essential pointer.

WHAT IS ILLUSORY?

Q: How do I tell what is illusory and what is real?

Wayne: The essential pointer of Advaita—which translates as "not-two"—is that everything is Consciousness. With the understanding that everything is One Consciousness, then how do we account for the multiplicity? One of the ways the multiplicity is talked about is to say that everything is an illusion. But that notion, as classical as it may be, is only part of the story.

It is not that the various objects are illusory. What is truly illusory is *the appearance of separation*, the sense that each object exists independently. This Living Teaching points to an underlying understanding in which each object is known to be an aspect of the One Consciousness, in no way separate. We as perceivers do not see the unity because it is the nature of the senses to objectify things, to quantify them and make them into discrete objects. That's what the senses do in order to know. So, the universe is illusory in that respect.

SPIRITUAL PROGRESS

Q: I've read the introduction to *Consciousness Speaks* where you talk a little about your relationship with your guru. After you began studying with Balsekar, did you just constantly question, "Who am I? Who am I? Who am I? Who is doing this?"

Wayne: No, it wasn't a formal process that I engaged in. I can tell you my own story, but it's just my story. It is not instructive in any way. When I met Ramesh, I essentially fell in love with him. I was drawn to him very much like a moth to a flame. There were all types of layers to this love, many of which were not of the purest and the highest. There were some very base desires at play: wanting attention, wanting recognition, wanting to connect to this incredible power so I could have it for myself. These were very personal kinds of desires. It was not an expansive, loving, generous, open kind of "wanting-to-give" energy. It wasn't that kind of love; it was grasping and acquiring.

However, the energy eventually shifted. That was the gift of this process: a movement away from an acquiring type of energy, to an expansive, wanting to give, be of service, how could I contribute energy. In that generous energy, there is freedom. The wanting to *get* it so I could *have* it was just spiritual materialism and more bondage.

It doesn't matter whether you're trying to get a thousand dollars, a bigger car, a bigger house, or more spiritual potency so that you can have more control; it's still a form of materialism. That's what the FSA is constantly concerned with, covering up its state of impotence with the trappings of power. As I spent more and more time with Ramesh and his teaching, the claiming power of the FSA seemed to just slip away and then, one day, it was completely gone.

~~~

Q: I still experience a slight feeling that there's something that can be attained.

Wayne: Yes, the attaining element is connected to the False Sense of Authorship. When you can author something, you can attain. So it's totally natural that this quality of attainment would accompany the sense of authorship.

Q: That's part of the human operating system, inherent in myself, right?

Wayne: No, it's part of most humans' experience because the FSA is present in most people. But it's not essential for the operation of the organism.

~~~

Q: You were talking about having a hole inside us that we are trying to fill with money, or fame, or spirituality. I have a sense of a hierarchy there. I think the guy who is concerned with making money will have less success at filling the hole than the guy who is trying a spiritual approach. But do you see it as exactly the same?

Wayne: It is all exactly the same. I don't consider the spiritual attempt to fill that hole to have any more value than to want to fill it with money or fame, or anything else.

Q: It's the same, psychologically?

Wayne: It's the same process, and it is one that is always doomed to failure. The hole you try to fill is open at the bottom.

THE FINAL ANSWER

Q: Wayne, what if my inquiry rests on the belief that there is a final answer, and that I'm waiting for you or somebody to tell me the answer…

Wayne: Fourteen. The final answer is Fourteen.

Q: ...but I see the seeking...

Wayne: What! You're not satisfied? You said you were waiting for me to give you the final answer, I gave you the final answer, and you're still not satisfied! [laughter]

Q: That's my *point*.

Wayne: That's *my* point.

Q: So, I'll continue to show up at different *satsangs* so that I get some other answer?

Wayne: You continue to show up at different *satsangs* because the universe moves you there. The story you tell about it is, "I'm not satisfied with various answers. My mind demands this and that"—that's the story that is self-serving in that it puts you at the center of this vast happening. You're being moved from here to there to there, and the way that you talk about that is about *your* having done it, through *your* interest, *your* curiosity, *your* demands, *your* efforts. It all comes back to Mark. What the Living Teaching is asking is, does it, *in fact,* come back to and then end with Mark? Or is Mark simply a single aspect of a much bigger whole?

SECTION
FIVE:
HUMAN PROCESSES

WORKING MIND, THINKING MIND

Q: Would you say, Wayne, that in your case the thinking mind is absent, and that you deal exclusively with the working mind?

Wayne: Yes, the FSA, or what Ramesh calls the "thinking mind," is absent. There is no longer that secondary involvement, that claiming process. It simply doesn't occur.

Q: Do you not project things into the future and worry about the consequences, about whether it will work out or not work out?

Wayne: Only in the practical sense. What Ramesh calls the "working mind" makes practical projections into the future and makes plans accordingly. Some people are planners, and others are more spontaneous, non-planning kind of people. The degree to which one actively plans has to do with the nature of the organism, not any kind of spiritual attainment. After Enlightenment there is an *absence of involvement* in what the organism does. There isn't any kind of enlightened *behavior*. Behavior is a product of the programming of the organism.

Q: Let's take a specific example so I can understand it better: if you think about the future, and whether there is enough money for retirement, and let's say you don't have enough money now, do you project into the future? When you think about what is needed for retirement, do you worry that you may not have enough? Is that a thinking mind example?

Wayne: The worry and fear for the future is a projected concern on the part of the FSA—"If I don't manage my future properly, what will become of *me*?"—not the practical consideration of what will happen physically, but what will become of "me." It is that projected fear which does not arise after Enlightenment, because there is no authoring "me" to be concerned. So the sage may calculate how much money will possibly be needed in the future to continue to live in the house he likes, and he may make plans to save accordingly. What is absent in the sage is the fear and anxiety people often experience around their inability to control the outcomes of their plans.

Q: So the involvement stops in the sage?

Wayne: Correct, there is no involvement, there is simply action, the action which is a product of the programming of the organism. And as long as the organism is alive it will breathe, it will act, it will think, it will feel. It may even plan for retirement.

BRAIN AND MIND

Q: When the sage offers a response to a question, there is the mind-body organism that the sage is associated with, and we are educated to understand that there is a mind in that complex which, through electrical impulses, creates thought.

Wayne: I don't know if we've determined whether electrical impulses actually create thought. It's the *mechanism* through which the thought is carried. But what the *origin* of the thought is seems to be still quite a mystery.

Q: It occurs to me that even the concept of the brain being potentially the origin of some thought, is in itself a thought. So it can't be a place where thought starts.

Wayne: An interesting thought.

WHO IS THINKING?

Q: My mind wants to know, what is true? I know I can never know the Truth but my mind keeps at it...

Wayne: The mind's activity *happens*. You're saying the mind wants to know. What is really happening is thoughts arise. You then assign causes to it. But, really, you're simply describing that thoughts arise. Thoughts arise, sometimes with a desire to understand and to know your true nature. These are seeker-thoughts. Most people are not having these kinds of thoughts. But certain humans are programmed in such a way that these thoughts are pursued and so there's an ongoing interest in them.

~~~

Q: So the sage just sits back and experiences life and Enlightenment?

Wayne: No. Now you're talking about the organism. The organism experiences life. It's not the organism that is Enlightened.

Q: At that point then, isn't it much like an animal doing whatever it does out in the wild?

Wayne: Absolutely. It is precisely like an animal in the wild, to the extent that there is no secondary involvement in what has happened.

Q: It does what it does naturally to exist on the planet.

Wayne: It does what it does. It does what it's programmed to do. That's what *every* organism does, be it human, or animal, or vegetable, whether there is Enlightenment or not. Most humans have something additional, which is this false claim that all that is be-ing done is "my" doing. That's laid on top of everything that's already happening. This claim is unique to humanity.

Q: So all that's happening is that we're along for the ride?

Wayne: There is no "we" along for the ride. There *is* only the ride. The ride is *happening.*

~~~

Q: Do you still have experiences where your mind starts gnawing away at some question or thought? And if you do, do you just let it run its course?

Wayne: I have an active mind, and my mind has, I think, the full range of human experience. There is never a question of either letting it run its course, or feeling that it shouldn't be doing what it's doing. There is simply the activity of the mind, just as there is the activity of the body and of the emotions. Those things *happen.*

~~~

Q: I can watch the thoughts come and go endlessly within my mind. Even the great ideas, I realize, are not mine; rather, they appear to me from somewhere. However, I *then* choose to act or not to act depending on which thoughts I choose to pursue.

Wayne: You can't have it both ways. The choice to pursue something is a thought, "I'm going to pursue this, I'm going to pursue that." But you already said the thoughts come and go, you can't control them, so which is it?

~~~

Q: Are you saying that our thoughts are ours, or do they simply arise—are we the author of our thoughts?

Wayne: I'm not telling you that you are the author or that you're not. What I'm doing is inviting you to *look* at that very essential question, to see if you *are* the creator of your thoughts. If you discover you *are* the author of your thoughts, then I assume you will only author nice, generous, kind and loving thoughts. You will no longer have any more of those mean, egotistical, nasty, ugly thoughts. But if you look honestly and find that you don't exercise that kind of control, the question of authorship begins to loom larger, "Am I really the author of my thoughts? If I am the author, how is it that these nasty, ugly thoughts come in?" I encourage you to look into it because the implications are huge.

YOU DON'T HAVE TO LIKE IT

Q: I'm at a place right now where I feel that there is nothing essentially that I can do to become what I already am. I don't feel I have any direction to go, any talk to attend, anything to do to get where I want to go. So at some level, I'm very resigned to the fact that it doesn't matter if I come here and listen to Wayne speak, or if I read this or that book. I'm very resigned to the fact that there's nothing I can do. But it is a bit bothersome, because I feel nothing I do can make any difference. I still have problems, I have suffering, and this acceptance you're talking about just ain't there. I've got this cat that's got chronic renal failure, and I'm not okay with that. And there are a lot of things that I'm not okay with, and I don't know where to go.

Wayne: The cat has renal failure, and that hurts you. That you don't like it is also part of What Is. That you will do whatever you can to make the cat more comfortable is also a part of What Is. The whole process is unfolding as part of the functioning of the Source. So, when we talk about acceptance of What Is, such acceptance *includes not liking it*, not being okay with it. Acceptance does not mean approval.

Q: And it includes my efforts to make the cat more comfortable?

Wayne: Absolutely. And the same would apply to whatever it is you do to "reach enlightenment" or to eliminate suffering. Those things also happen as part of the functioning of the Source. We can say that the "reason" these things are happening is because they are part of the Totality of Being. When that Understanding is reached, then the dissatisfaction you are feeling and the resignation will be gone. Resignation is a reflection of a feeling of *limited* power, not total powerlessness. The recognition of one's *total* power-lessness is freedom. There is a transcendent shift between feeling that you have limited power, and Enlightenment, that is total powerlessness.

LOSING A LOVED ONE

Q: I've been suffering very much spiritually. My twenty-one year old son died a couple years ago and it knocked me out.

Wayne: I am truly sorry for your loss.

My guru, Ramesh Balsekar, is an Enlightened Master. I was with him in 1989 when he was in the States on a speaking tour and news came to him that his son had died in Bombay. His grief was enormous, of course. People have a fantasy that when there is Enlightenment there is no longer any pain. It is imagined that everything becomes fine, beautiful, sweet and light all the time. That's not true. Life is, by its very nature, exquisitely beautiful and exquisitely painful. Someone more poetic than me said it is like licking honey off a thorn.

As long as there is life in the human organism we call the sage, there will be experiences of beauty and horror, joy and sorrow.

What we can call the blessing of Enlightenment is that there is no suffering attendant to the pain. There is not the slightest sense that things as they are, no matter how painful, should be different, or that what has happened should not have happened. There is the implicit understanding that everything that happens is part of a massive functioning, part of a huge tapestry of Totality. Whatever has happened is understood to have been inescapable. It could not have been otherwise. In that Acceptance, there is peace even in the most profound grief, or the most profound pain.

DEATH

Q: When this human organism dies, what happens to it? Is it absorbed back into What Is?

Wayne: The organism was never separate from What Is. You can't be absorbed back into something you were never separate from. What actually happens is that when the human organism dies, the surrounding human organisms hasten to get rid of it. It becomes a nuisance very quickly. Burn it or bury it, or leave it out for the birds to eat; do something with it!

Once the body is disposed of, then everybody can get on with their grief and their life. The organism itself returns to its constituent elemental parts. The elemental molecules of the body will be recycled into other organisms, and perhaps become part of other life forms.

That's what happens to the body but is the body what you are? That's the real question.

SEX

Q: Sexual orgasm is very satisfying. Is it because there is no authorship during that moment?

Wayne: I would say that the intensity of the orgasmic experience precludes involvement by the FSA, yes. But it is not the absence of involvement by the FSA which makes the orgasm what it is. It's a much more complex physical response. If the absence of the authoring "me" was the equivalent of the orgasm, the sage would be walking around with a silly little smile on his or her face all the time.

SECTION SIX: FEELINGS

EMOTIONS

Q: Do your feelings get hurt?

Wayne: Absolutely.

Q: And then what happens?

Wayne: When my feelings get hurt, I experience emotional pain. And when my body gets hurt, I experience physical pain.

Q: And you don't identify with the emotional pain?

Wayne: What do you mean by "identify with" it?

Q: There is no involvement with the hurt feelings?

Wayne: Correct. There simply are hurt feelings. And it's not an *impersonal* hurt feeling; I, Wayne, have my feelings hurt, because I, Wayne, am a functional organism that has human characteristics. And that human organism continues to function even after Enlightenment. The FSA, as I call it, is something that is laid on top of that basic human functioning. This "claiming me" falsely claims to be the author of the thoughts, feelings and actions that happen through the body and mind. It is that involvement which is suffering.

In this Living Teaching we make a distinction between pain and suffering. Pain is what happens physically or emotionally in the moment. Suffering is when that happening of the moment is extended into the past and the future by the FSA's involvement, "It shouldn't have happened this way," "How will I cope if it continues this way?" Such concerns are suffering.

Q: So does it all just stop in one fell swoop, or do you exert some effort to detach yourself from it?

Wayne: There is no personal effort whatsoever, because there is no one to exert that effort to detach.

ANGER

Q: Isn't anger a secondary involvement, a FSA involvement?

Wayne: No, not necessarily. It is a reaction.

Q: Who is feeling the anger?

Wayne: The same person who just asked the question.

Q: When I look at anger, when it arises, I see there is also a sense of "this shouldn't be."

Wayne: That may well be an add-on to the anger. But the anger itself can be a reaction by the *organism* to that which it doesn't like—"should" or "shouldn't" need not be involved at all. There can simply be a response of not liking something, even *intensely* not liking something. Certain people are programmed to react with anger in situations that they don't like. Others may display no more than mild irritation. Still others may show no visible reaction at all. A wonderful example of this was my guru's guru, Nisargadatta Maharaj, who was very quick to display anger—red faced, veins-popping-out-in-the-head kind of anger. People were often quite taken aback and they would ask, "Maharaj, why do you get so angry?" His response was, "Who is angry? There *is* anger. There is anger, and *it* expresses. There is no *one* who is angry."

Q: But isn't the arising of anger dependent on a point of view?

Wayne: Of course it is.

Q: Well, doesn't that mean, then, that if anger arises it automatically means that there is FSA-involvement?

Wayne: No.

Q: Isn't a point of view, an opinion about this and that, a result of FSA-involvement?

Wayne: No, a point of view is a function of the organism. If there is a functioning human being, he's going to have a point of view, and he's going to have preferences. He's going to have likes and dislikes because the human being is a programmed instrument. If he is programmed not to be masochistic, he will prefer to be stroked gently and lovingly, rather than be tortured with a hot, sharp instrument. So we say he has a preference. There is a peculiar notion that after Enlightenment the body-mind apparatus no longer has preferences; love it, torture it, it doesn't matter, it doesn't care, you can do anything you want to it— it's thought to have become a lifeless, non-responsive lump of human tofu. Another popular model is that it becomes a *beatific* lump of tofu that only has positive qualities—in accordance with the relative scale of positive qualities used by the person making the description, of course.

But, in fact, what we're talking about is a human apparatus, a human organism that will likely shy away from pain by its very nature, and be attracted to pleasure by its nature. Likes and dislikes are very much a part of the personality of the organism; without a personality the organism is bland and lifeless. It is the personality that becomes angry, in the moment, according to its nature. Consider the conduct of two widely recognized Enlightened beings: Nisargadatta Maharaj's personality was one in which he often responded to that which he didn't like with anger whereas Ramana Maharshi's personality was one in which there was rarely a display of anger. The absence or presence of anger was not a measure of spiritual attainment, but simply an example of the difference in the programming of the organism itself.

ANXIETY

Q: When I look deeply into myself, I often come across a certain tension around that looking, and there is anxiety there.

Wayne: So, when you look and find the tension there, go another level deeper into the tension, to see from where it arises. If the tension is there, presumably it exists. Where does it abide, and how does it relate to you?

Q: It seems to be sort of floating there. It's not really connected to much.

Wayne: It may well be floating. But if it's really floating there and not connected to much, then it has no more significance to you than the dust mote that just went by. The dust mote went by, but you don't really give a damn about that at this moment. But the tension has a component that connects to "you."

Q: That's true. There seems to be a concern for myself there at some level.

Wayne: I can only encourage you to continue to look deeply, and when you get to that point where the only thing there is this amorphous anxiety—look at it—what is it connected to? How does it relate to "me"?

~~~

Q: How do you make thirty-four years of decisions look like they never were decisions? How do you see that they just happened and stop worrying about what you're going to do, and just let it happen!

Wayne: The worrying *also* simply happens! You aren't initiating the worry. The worrying is part of the same happening, the anxiety is part of the same happening, and the letting go is part of the same happening.

~~~

Q: So what exactly is anxiety?

Wayne: I would say that you know what anxiety is! [laughter]

Q: True, what is the cause of anxiety, then?

Wayne: Anxiety has multiple causes. Presumably, behind the question is the belief that if you can know what's causing it, you can figure out how to eliminate the cause, and so eliminate the anxiety. This is a therapeutic approach, which may have validity in some contexts; however, this Living Teaching is not one of them. Here we're looking at the whole question from another angle. Perhaps, upon looking, you will see that anxiety ultimately arises as part of the functioning of Totality. When there is acceptance of the Whole, then that includes an acceptance of whatever anxiety may arise. Within the acceptance is peace, and the peace can coexist with anxiety.

Q: So are you saying anger precedes the thinking that *I'm* angry because things should be different to the way they are?

Wayne: That is correct. After Enlightenment, anger is a direct response, in the moment, by the organism. There is no add-on of FSA-involvement such as "I should have" or "I shouldn't have."

RESPONSIBILITY

Q: Isn't this Living Teaching just another way to avoid responsibility?

Wayne: What we talk about as "responsibility" is a social construct. "Responsibility" relates to a socially dictated set of standards. When your actions are in line with the standard, you say, "I was being responsible," meaning I met the expectations of my society. If you have internalized that expectation, you say, "I am responsible to myself," meaning you're meeting your own expectations. The real question is—how is it that you (a) care about it in the first place, and (b) are given the strength to act accordingly? Obviously, this ability to act responsibly is given to certain people and not others. Certain people don't care, and we call those people "irresponsible." The question the Living Teaching raises is, *what* is responsible for the creation of responsible acts, and *what* is responsible for the creation of irresponsible acts?

Q: Ramesh frequently uses the concept that nothing matters or "Who cares?" This is a useful pointer to the Absolute, but when applied to the world of appearance, this concept can bring about a detached, heartless person who doesn't think that they should care or work towards change, even if they feel the impulse to do so. The thought "nothing matters" shuts down the caring heart because one now thinks they should take on this thought if they want Enlightenment.

Wayne: Students of the Living Teaching sometimes mistakenly conclude that *nothing* matters. It's as if the FSA were saying, "If I'm not doing it, then nothing has any value." But that's not the Living Teaching. The Living Teaching says that whether something matters or not is a relative consideration. When Ramesh says, "Who cares?!" in the title of his book, that has a double meaning. The questions the Living Teaching invites you to explore are: Who is caring? What is the source of caring? Is it the individual, or is it the Vital Force? What is it that makes one person "responsible" and another "irresponsible"?

~~~

Q: What about making promises, judgments and requests? What about promising your daughter you will be there for her graduation, or she'll be picked up

from school, or assessing whether a particular sur-
geon can be trusted to perform surgery on a loved
one? Somehow, even if "you aren't there," these
promises are being made; these assessments are being performed. To say that Consciousness is doing
it—well if I'm your daughter, I can't kick Consciousness' ass if it fails to pick me up and I'm left standing
in the rain, and obviously, assessments are being
made. So clearly, a sage makes complex judgments,
but if no-one is there, who makes these assessments?
If no-one is there, who is accountable, and who makes
promises such that you're on time for this talk?

Wayne: This question points to a basic misinterpreta-
tion of the Living Teaching. Clearly the things you
mentioned happen, and the organism we call the sage
makes complicated assessments. As you said, the *organism* does that. In the pointer that "there's no-one
there," who do you imagine is the "one" that's being
talked about, the one who isn't there? Obviously,
something is there which is functioning. It may be functioning in ways you like or in ways you don't like,
but something is definitely there. In the sage, there is
something that *isn't* there, that is presumably there in
the rest of people. So what is it?

The term I use to point precisely to this, is "the
False Sense of Authorship," which is synonymous
with what people often talk about as the "ego" or the
"me." There is a claiming to be the author of the various acts that actually happen as part of the functioning
of Totality. When we say that in the sage there is no-
one there, we mean there is no authoring entity
existent. There is no FSA.

In this Living Teaching, you are encouraged to try and find that sense of authorship. You have an *a priori* belief that it exists, a belief that "I am the author," but is it true? Is that truly what is happening?"

It is the human organism, which is a product of its genetics and its conditioning, which makes promises and breaks promises. The *organism* is what behaves—it behaves well, or it behaves badly. The organism behaves well or badly, and it gets credit or blame—but even the credit or the blame isn't necessarily linked to the behavior. People get promoted or demoted all the time for work that their sub-ordinates did. People get convicted of crimes they never committed and other people commit crimes and are never caught for them. So yes, there are results to actions, but the results aren't even necessarily linked to the actions themselves, in any directly causal way.

For this Living Teaching to have value, you must look deeply into what I am pointing to. I know I am throwing a lot at you at once, but there is no hurry. Consider these pointers at your leisure. See if they fit. See if they have any relevance.

COMPASSION

Q: In discussions about compassion, I often see that compassion is interpreted as an expression of empathy. But in thinking further about empathy, it seems to me that empathy requires the involvement of a self in the suffering of another and, if that self is involved, the empathy has the quality of, "I've felt this kind of suffering that you're feeling and, therefore, I share your pain." So it seems, when you look at it that way, that empathy may be a contributor to future suffering.

Wayne: No, this is where you're getting a little confused, because when you talk about the self, there are two aspects of the self. Often we have discussions in these kinds of teachings about being relieved of the self, that the self is the source of the separation, and that the sage has been relieved of this self-ness. But we have to be careful, because the "self" that these teachings pointing at, is what I call the "FSA self." But there is also a functional self, which is what feels empathy. Empathy is a human trait. Human beings usually have the capacity for empathy as part of their programming. The human, functional self, is what operates regardless of whether or not there is a "false authoring me" present, though it generally operates a lot more smoothly when the FSA is absent.

Q: So compassion and empathy are expressions that occur within the phenomenal experience?

Wayne: Correct, empathy is a phenomenal response, and people feel empathy in accordance with their nature. Some people are far more empathetic than others. True Compassion, the Compassion of the sage, is synonymous with Total Acceptance. It isn't empathy with someone for some situation, which is normally what is thought of as compassion. It is empathy for what they are as a perfect expression of the Source. True Compassion is Total, not relative.

Q: What is an act of compassion?

Wayne: You will get considerable disagreement about that. As far as I'm concerned, no *act* is an indicator of compassion. Any act is simply an act; there are kind ones and there are unkind ones. The difference is not always readily apparent. We'll take the example of a four-year-old child with a razor-sharp knife in her hand. She's having a great time swinging this knife around. Then you come and take the knife away from her and her response is to scream at you because you've taken her toy away. From the child's point of view, it is not perceived to be a kind act. So is it a kind act or not? It depends who you ask. It depends on the perspective. All we can really say is that it is an act—which is then given significance and is judged by whoever perceives it.

Q: Ramesh referred to the deepest and truest form of compassion as that which is Consciousness itself—an expression of Consciousness, I can't quite remember how he put it...

Wayne: Total Acceptance—which is an act without a subsequent claim of involvement, whatever the act.

Q: That would get me in a lot of trouble with the Buddhists.

Wayne: Of course it would. It would get you in trouble with a lot of religious people. Every group has a code of behavior that is used to measure if an act conforms to the values of that group. And that is what is used to determine if something is compassionate or good. Rarely is the code of behavior questioned, or its relative nature examined and acknowledged.

GREED

Wayne: On Saturday, towards the end of the webcast, people were tuning in, and were complaining that they weren't able to get the feed. It turns out that someone had decided to attempt to download 25 videos off of the website, all at once, and sucked up all the bandwidth we have here. Nothing else was able to get through. It's astonishing how greed extends into every avenue, whether it's greed for money, for power, or for "spiritual" things. [laughter] There is an impulse to acquire, to get things for oneself. This is all part of the dance of life. We have, on the one hand, the generosity of a person who donates to make the webcasts possible, and on the other hand a person whose nature is to take as much as they can, as fast as they can. Life itself is the incredible mixture of people and attitudes and desires.

It often comes as a surprise to people that the real satisfaction in life is in generosity, not in acquisition. The inherent problem with acquisition is that you can never acquire enough. Once you've "got it," there's always more to get, and so it's an endless emptiness. Whatever satisfaction one gets upon obtaining something is always incredibly brief and temporary. You can see this by looking at your own life: the moments when there is generosity, when there is giving, when there is openness—it feels great! You feel better about yourself, you feel better about the world, and everything's wonderful. But despite that, even when you can *see* the obvious benefits, you can't *make* yourself different from how you are. You can't force yourself to be other than you are, even when you see it's ultimately in your own best interests! [laughter]

Here, once again, we have evidence of the fact that we're not determining our lives. If we were, we would all act very differently. The greatest blessing of this Living Teaching is the seeing that comes with the deepening of understanding. We may come to see that we are as we are because of forces vastly greater than our desires or our intentions. How we are in this moment is not our self-authored doing, is not a product of our self-authored efforts.

Everybody will come up short when measuring their actions against their values. Everybody comes up short when comparing their actuality against their ideal of what an ideal person, an ideal life, and an ideal response should be.

If you're burdened with the idea that you are the architect of your existence, and you take stock of yourself, there is inevitably a sense of failure. There is a sense of being less than what you *should* be, of being inadequate, of not doing it well enough. The only way out of that trap is through a deeper understanding in which it becomes clear that what you truly are in your essence, is an aspect of the Universal Life Force.

Each of us is a product of millennia of natural selection coded into our DNA, combined with the influences of the conditions into which we are thrust after we are born. Once there is an understanding of this rudimentary fact, then further investigation into the essential nature of things can more readily take place. But until this understanding comes you will be fully occupied trying to engineer your life. It takes an enormous amount of physical and psychic energy to try to exert your will on the Totality of Existence. It's exhausting at every level of being.

GUILT

Wayne: One of the most interesting places to look and perhaps catch a glimpse of what we are calling the FSA, is in what you feel guilty about. If you feel guilty about something, then inevitably, that guilt is a result of the sense that "I," as this entity, was the author of that which I feel guilty about. If you were simply the *instrument* of it, then guilt would not arise. There might be regret that an event happened, but there would not be any more guilt over that occurrence than there would be guilt over the fact that a hurricane went through New Orleans. You don't feel guilty about the hurricane; even though you may regret that it happened.

Q: Right.

Wayne: With the understanding that what happens *through* you is not *sourced* by you, guilt has no place from which to arise, even when the outcome is terrible. When there is guilt, it is a clear indicator that there is an active sense of authorship, and it is there that you might concentrate your attention. Investigate the underpinnings of this guilt. That I feel guilty about something must mean I was the source of it. Is that assumption true?

Q: Yeah, that makes total sense, the whole feeling of "Why didn't I get more done today? I should have done more!"—that is very pervasive in my life.

Wayne: Yes, it can be summed up in the one word: *should*—"I *should* have done more. I *should* have done better. I *should* not have done what I did." So it's that quality of *should*-ness that we're looking into, as an indicator of the presence of the FSA. Perhaps by looking more deeply into that, a revelatory understanding about the true nature of what is operative may happen. It isn't inquiring or studiously examining the issue in order to get an answer, so much as it is looking for the sake of looking, then seeing what comes out of that. Simple curiosity is all that is required.

~~~

Q: At some kind of broad level it makes sense to me that my actions are part of the functioning of Totality, but it is hard to see how it applies to all decisions.

Wayne: It is indeed difficult to see what genetic and environmental factors are operating in the decision to move your hand from here to there. That is why we don't use that as a window into the process, it is too obscure. What I point to, as often being the clearest window into the process, is to look at something that you feel guilty about.

As the Living Teaching has its impact on you, it changes you. The change it engenders carries with it a reduction of guilt, because the change is a weakening of the FSA, and it is the FSA that produces guilt with its claim that "I authored it." It is a direct connection; if you didn't author an action, no guilt could accrue. You might regret that it happened, you might be really sorry to see that something unpleasant occurred, but guilt can only result from a sense that you produced the action, that you were the source of it.

THERE'S SOMETHING WRONG WITH ME

Q: I feel bad about myself. I feel like I don't love people enough, and I'm too selfish.

Wayne: I believe that's a genuine feeling—you feel that you're not loving enough, or that you're selfish, or concerned with your own...

Q: I'm too self-absorbed.

Wayne: Okay, so let's assume that you are self-absorbed, to whatever degree—we'll leave the "too" out of it. If we start there and work backwards to the source of the self-absorption, how is it that Sheila has become self-absorbed? Did you one day decide, "I think I'm going to be self-absorbed today"?

Q: No.

Wayne: No? So the self-absorption *happened*.

Q: Yeah, little by little.

Wayne: Okay, little by little, and we'll assume there's some genetic predisposition to self-absorption, and some sort of quality in your body that may enable you to be self-absorbed. Then your experiences in life, little by little, may have fostered an increase in self-absorption. Now, the real question is, did *you* engineer those events in your life that may have increased the self-absorption?

Q: I think so. I have to take responsibility, right?

Wayne: We're just asking questions here—there are no right or wrong answers. This Living Teaching encourages you to find the truth for yourself, by looking into your own experience. In the course of your life, experiences happen. The real question is what was *your* part in bringing those experiences into being? If you deconstruct any event in your life, you may begin to see that any singular event is part of a much larger and more complex matrix than what you could possibly create with your own physical being. If you can look at your own experience and your own background, you may begin to see that how you are in this moment, is a product of vast genetic and environmental forces beyond the possibility of personal control.

If you look, and you see that these genetic and environmental forces were responsible for creating who you are today, then guilt eases naturally, on its own. You don't have to make any efforts to reduce it; it simply dissipates in the seeing.

We're all a mixed bag of qualities. If any of us were capable of creating our own beingness, we would all be saints! We would be loving and kind and generous all the time, because when we're loving and kind and generous we feel better; everybody feels better, and it brings more joy into life. The fact that despite our best intentions and our most earnest observations and efforts we're still filled with positive and negative qualities, seems to suggest a certain lack of control on the part of the human organism. Perhaps, if you look, you will see deeply into the mystery and be freed from this crushing burden of guilt, blame and shame.

HOPE

Q: When my seeking was intense, there was lots of suffering. But now the seeking for Enlightenment has become greatly reduced. I'm not really sure why. However, it's hard living without that hope. I thought that when the seeking for Enlightenment eased up, things would improve. What's the deal?

Wayne: *This* is the deal. *This* is what's happening. In this moment, there is hopelessness happening. Previously, there was intense seeking for Enlightenment, and then the intensity of the seeking diminished. The hope obviously remained strong that the fruits of the seeking would be sweet, and from that expectation came disappointment. That's the deal. That's what's happening. But what happens in the next moment, we'll have to see. So if we talk again in a few weeks, everything could be quite different for you. We'll have to see.

~~~

Q: Wayne, you give me some anticipation and hope for something better. Can this hope be an obstacle?

Wayne: Certainly, it can be an obstacle, or it can be a facilitator. We'll have to see what happens. Then we can say whether the hope helped, or the hope hurt. All we can really say for now is that the hope is *happening*. With the simple recognition that the hope is happening, there's no problem, there's peace.

LOVE

Q: Would you have any recommendations in order to have healthy relationships without the craziness of my ego involvement?

Wayne: I'm on my third marriage, so you probably don't want to take relationship advice from me! [laughter]

Q: And knowing what you know now?

Wayne: Knowing what I know now, my recommendation is: love more, give more, without any expectations of getting anything.

Q: Just live like that all the time?

Wayne: Yes, if you can. [laughter] That's the big kicker: *if you can*. And if you can't, understand that it is simply not within your power at this moment to live that way.

SECTION SEVEN: PERSONAL CONCERNS

AM I LISTENING TO THE RIGHT VOICE?

Q: Could I make the wrong decisions? I am afraid I could be going against the grain?

Wayne: When you say, "make the wrong decisions" what do you mean?

Q: Well, say the universe is unfolding through me in a certain direction, but I seem to have a tendency to go against it.

Wayne: The fundamental question is, *can* you go against the will of the Universe? Where do you stand, relative to the totality of the Universe, to go against it? If you're *part* of it, then it's like standing in your own boots and trying to lift yourself up by the boot-straps; how do you do it?

MAKING DECISIONS

Q: Are you saying that I merely *think* that I'm making the decisions?

Wayne: You certainly *do* make decisions, and you *must* make decisions.

Q: So what's the difference between what you're saying and making decisions?

Wayne: The essential distinction I'm making is between the *doing,* and the *authoring.* So, certainly, decisions have to be made. The question is, what is the source of the decision? Are you the instrument *through which* decisions are being made, or are you the *author* of the decisions?

When the "me" is present, its sole job is to claim authorship for any choice that happens. When the "me" is involved, you will have the sense, "I choose, and I am the source of the choosing," and this will produce the anxiety associated with making the right choices. There will be fear over how the outcome will affect "me."

ACCEPTANCE

Q: I am aware of the value of being present and yet, as much as I make resolutions to be present, I can't seem to stay present. So I just try to accept that I can't, but even that acceptance doesn't last.

Wayne: That's true, but the acceptance you are talking about is a conditional acceptance, a relative acceptance, and such acceptances are *always* short-lived. They are a dualistic movement, so you move from a state of "I accept this," to a state of "I don't accept this." The seed of non-acceptance is inherent in the dualistic type of acceptance.

When we talk about Acceptance in a bigger sense, the Acceptance that we're talking about is non-dual and unconditional. This capitalized Acceptance is a non-dual acceptance, meaning it's Total. It is not *you* accepting something else such as, "I'm accepting that my mate is inconsiderate." That kind of specific acceptance is relative; some *one* is accepting some *thing*. Acceptance of What Is is inclusive of everything—everything, including the acceptance and non-acceptance that are relative and transient. That's a crucial thing to keep in mind when we're using these terms.

Q: That conjures an image in my head of a candle reflected a million times in a mirror: accepting that, accepting that I accept that, and then accepting that I accept that I accept that, and never ending the duality of that acceptance.

Wayne: Yes, you're absolutely correct. It is an infinite regression. The only way out of that is Transcendence, which is what the mystics have been pointing at for millennia. Transcendence is the movement beyond the limitations of the duality. But, even subtler than that, it is a shift from something to Nothing—not a nihilistic nothing, not a vast, empty, dark hole of a nothing, but Nothing which is the source of everything. This transcendent movement from the dualistic awareness, to a mystical, or a holistic Awareness, is all-inclusive and beyond all possible concepts of It. The problem in *talking* about such things is that, inevitably, when you talk about a transcendent awareness, the only way you can conceptualize it is dualistically; there is no escaping this.

Q: *"The Tao that can be named..."*

Wayne: *"The Tao that can be named is not the true Tao,"* yes. Lao Tzu had it right.

LIKES AND DISLIKES

Q: In a state of Enlightenment, do liking and not-liking feel like the same thing?

Wayne: Liking and not-liking are a function of the programming of the organism. Each human organism is constructed to like and dislike certain things. There is a basic genetic predisposition to be attracted to certain things, and repelled by others, as part of being human. Additionally, as part of your enculturation, you will be attracted to certain things and not others. In certain cultures, if you find a grub underneath the tree bark and pop it into your mouth and chew on it, it's your lucky day. If in California you're handed that same grub and you're told to eat it, you're probably not going to experience that as a blessing.

Q: Whether there is Enlightenment or not?

Wayne: Exactly. It has nothing to do with Enlightenment. The body isn't enlightened. The body is meat. The meat has a certain genetic predisposition and subsequent environmental conditioning. In this equation, genetics plus conditioning equals programming. The programming is dynamic; it is changing every instant. You react a certain way in this instant, then two seconds later, after other circumstances have occurred, the programming becomes different, and you may react completely differently. The reaction, in the moment, is a function of the programming of the organism. What sometimes follows is that the FSA then falsely claims the functioning as a product of *its* doing.

BEING IN CONTROL

Q: Does suffering begin because you feel you have control? I think the clearest I've ever been regarding suffering, is when you said something about feeling pain—that *pain is, it exists*, but when one says that pain shouldn't be, then there is suffering. You also said the suffering begins with the FSA. Can you walk me through that?

Wayne: The "me" that is claiming authorship or control is essentially insecure. It must be essentially insecure because at some level it knows that its claim of having power is false. The schizoid part of this process is that the claim of control is made adamantly, while at the same time there is the understanding that "I must not have enough power, otherwise I would be able to control everything all the time." This tacit knowledge underlies the false claim. Therefore, there is always a discomfort surrounding the claim.

Q: Vulnerability, so to speak.

Wayne: Yes, the vulnerability that comes with living a lie. The claim of authorship is a lie. It's unsupportable, and yet it's there. That's where the conflict and the insecurity are set up.

The mechanics of the suffering itself, is the taking of an essentially painful event in the moment, then extending it into the past and the future as it relates to "me." How will I cope? What will its impact be on "me"—not the organism-me, but "me," the false claimant? It is this projection out of the moment that is the difference between pain and suffering.

Q: And it's the part that Ramesh says is totally unnecessary.

Wayne: When he says it's not necessary, he means that it can happen in another way; it isn't the only way things can occur. If it happened, he would say it was necessary. It couldn't have been other than it was, but it can be other than it was in the next heartbeat.

Q: The teaching could have an effect beyond my control because everything is beyond my control? And even this knowing is beyond my control?

Wayne: Exactly.

Q: That seems like it's not a bad thing—but then who am I? Nothing? There's no control? Whenever I get to that point, I get a strange feeling like, "Then what am I?"

Wayne: If you look deeply into that, you'll find that your frustration is not in the complete lack of control, but in the partial lack. There is still a false claim of authorship there. The Living Teaching is emasculating it. It is getting weaker, but it's still there.

~~~

Q: I fear that the Universal Life Force is not on my side. I know it's supposed to be neutral and it doesn't really care about me, but that scares me and I don't feel safe. You know what I mean?

Wayne: Yes, I do know what you mean, and you're absolutely right. The world is not safe, and this quest for security and a sense of safety in this very unsafe world carries with it the seed of fear, because it is so patently impossible to control everything! You can bar the doors and the windows, you can keep the world out, but you can't control a plane falling out of the sky and hitting your house. There is no way that you can control everything.

A different approach, one that may feel counterintuitive, is to realize there *is* no safety, there *are* no guarantees, and there is no way you can control life. When that happens, there is peace. That's the irony. When the total surrender to whatever is going to happen, happens, there is peace.

Q: Does that, then, mean that bad or painful things won't happen?

Wayne: Of course not! But you may have noticed that even after a lifetime of attempting to keep difficult and painful experiences away, they have still occurred. They have come despite your very best efforts! When you see that pain and difficulty are inescapable aspects of human life, the suffering that often accompanies them is diminished.

Q: What if you get more in touch with that Self, and less with the FSA? Then isn't that Self the creator of everything? So isn't there some communing with that Self which does create—I don't want to use the word "control"—but maybe then you have more co-creation?

Wayne: You may not want to use the word "control" but isn't that what you are talking about? Co-creation is a New Age fantasy that is a feast for the FSA. It is born out of a misunderstanding that sometimes follows the realization, "Consciousness is everything and thus, I am part of that Everything." Where it all goes tragically wrong is with the notion that when "I" recognize my Everything-ness, "I" can then tap into the power of Everything and then "I" (the FSA) can have control.

This is such a desirable place for the FSA, that says, "Okay, I'm not separate [winks], I'm actually

Consciousness [winks]." But the agenda is that when "I" get together with Everything, "I" will be taken care of, because once "I" am on the scene, "I" can then take care of "*me.*" It comes back to taking care of "*me,*" and so it isn't really Consciousness-creation, it's me-creation! [laughter] It's "me," hoping to somehow harness the power of God to create what "I" think is best. The FSA is still looking out for itself, but now in a spiritual guise; now it says, "I am co-creating with God to get what I want." And, of course, you are going to also be very generous and do things for the world as well. But when you get to the root of it, what are you *really* concerned with? The concern is with "me," identified with the body; *you* want to be healthy, you want to be loving, you want to be open, you want to be present, you want to be emotionally and physically pain-free, you want more love, you want more prosperity at every level and you want all this for your loved ones too.

The arrogant assumption in all of this is that Consciousness/God/Source needs your help in working out some of the finer details in the creation.

~~~

Wayne: The basic quest of the FSA for more power is endless and impossible to fulfill. So, the only real solution is in the dissolution of the FSA that is seeking power, and in that dissolution there is peace. But it is counter-intuitive, and the FSA screams, "Without me you're nothing! It's all gonna go to shit! You are going to be homeless, living on the street, digging through garbage cans, doing nothing. Without me in control, your decisions will all be crap! Or you won't make any decisions at all; you'll just sit there and drool!" [laughter] This is what the FSA will have you believe: "*I'm* responsible for everything! You get rid of me, and nothing's gonna happen anymore!"

We're joking about it, but that is the claim, and there is a profound fear that goes with a deep investigation into the claim of the FSA. It is a very deep fear of things spiraling out of "*my*" control. There is a fear that "I" won't be able to get what "I" want and what "I" think "I" need, and "I" will be miserable. The Living Teaching is concerned with exposing this lie.

Q: That the FSA is in control?

Wayne: That the FSA is in control, and that the FSA has your best interests at heart.

DESIRE AND RENUNCIATION

Q: Do you agree that even though there is no FSA in reality, there is still an appearance of a FSA that wants shelter, food, sex and an attractive shirt?

Wayne: The FSA is *not* what wants food, shelter, sex and attractive shirts; those desires are simply a result of the programming of the organism. Most human beings are designed to seek food, shelter and sex. Some are also programmed to seek attractive shirts. The FSA then becomes involved in the desire. It's a *secondary* involvement by the FSA.

Let's use sex as an example, since it's such a perennially popular subject. When the FSA becomes involved in sexual desire, the objective begins to go far beyond sex into the realm of personal satisfaction with life. The FSA makes an insidious promise, "If I get sex then I will feel not only satisfied, but I will, as the FSA, feel complete. If I get the object of my desire, I will feel personally satisfied and fulfilled." This no longer has very much to do with the sexual urge itself. When the primary sexual urge is satisfied, it is over and done. The desire by the FSA is *never* finished. There may be a momentary sense of fulfillment, but it is always followed by an even more intense desire for more. It is an endless process that is relentlessly disappointing.

The basic desire—whether it is for food, shelter, sex, recognition in society, or money—is simply a function of the organism. But the acquisition of those things will never satisfy the FSA, and so there is an ongoing state of dissatisfaction and suffering.

That's why I find the whole idea of renunciation fascinating. The strategy is that by renouncing the fruits of desire—you rid yourself of all worldly goods, you get rid of all your nice shirts, you stop having sex, you don't hold money, you eat only enough food to keep the organism alive—that this will bring you closer to Enlightenment. It is hoped that with renunciation, the FSA will no longer have any fuel to sustain itself. But the FSA is infinitely resourceful, and it simply says, with apparent modesty, "I am a renunciant, I am not concerned with the pleasure of earthly things, I am not the flesh, I am a simple seeker after Truth, that's what I am!" And so it remains alive and well fed.

SHOULD AND SHOULDN'T

Q: I know I should be meditating but I just won't do it. I can't seem to go through with it and I miss it.

Wayne: So if you miss it, why do you think it is that you don't do it?

Q: I wish I had the answer for that. I feel like I really should do it but somehow I don't get around to it.

Wayne: "Should" is a very interesting word and a very interesting feeling as well. It might be worth investigating the nature of that sentence, "I *should* be doing something other than what I am doing," because it stems from a presumption. It presumes that you are the source of the doing in the first place. Without that presumption, "should" makes no sense. "Should" is only applicable to the situation if you have some creative input to the situation. By creative, I mean that you, as an authoring entity, are capable of creating this action.

Q: It sounds like you're saying there's value in asking and wondering. So it seems to me it's better to ask than not to ask. But that also seems like it would mean you *should* ask, but we talked about there not being a "should." Is it better to ask than not to ask?

Wayne: Once again, the "should," is connected to this presumption of authorship. We can make an evaluation and say that one thing is better than another, based on our values, without an accompanying "should." From my standpoint, it is better to be gently loved than to be brutally assaulted, but that is different from feeling that the universe *should* only give me love, and not give me any pain or misery.

The "shoulds" that create suffering also arise out of the belief that you know what is right in an absolute sense. When you believe that your values are absolute and the universe delivers something out of step with your values, you are left with the horrible feeling that the universe is somehow out of order.

Q: So we can prefer things, but we should, we can't, we should… [laughter]…I'm sorry… but we can't *expect* that things go as we prefer?

Wayne: "Expect" is one way of putting it. It often goes deeper than that. When things go badly, meaning that they go in a direction that you don't like, it may feel like there is something fundamentally flawed in what has happened. You think, "God *shouldn't* have made the universe this way." That's the basis of suffering. You can not like what you did, or what somebody else did, or what happened, and it can stop there. When you simply say, "I like it" or "I don't like it" the field stays clean and clear because your preferences simply reflect your nature as a human organism. You don't like certain things and you do like other things, and when things happen you react according to whether you like them or you don't like them. That is not suffering. There may be tremendous pain in the moment when something you don't like happens, for example, when someone close to you dies or when you're unlucky in love. But the pain does not become suffering unless there is a sense that you should have done it differently, that they should have done it differently, or that the universe should have done it differently.

~~~

Q: If there is no "should" and "should not"—it seems that works on one level, but on another level, we have to live in the real world. In society there are things that you should and should not do. How do you reconcile that? At a head-level, I realize there is this non-duality and that things are One, but having to live in the real world…

Wayne: Yes, so let's look at living in the real world. Have you ever done anything that you felt you shouldn't?

Q: Sure, yeah.

Wayne: Okay, how does that happen?

Q: I don't know.

Wayne: That's a point that may be worth investigating. You say that in order to live in the real world, you need to have these "shoulds" and "shouldn'ts" in order to control your behavior? But what you're telling me is that you already *have* "shoulds" and "shouldn'ts," and despite that you do things that you feel you shouldn't.

Q: If I'm doing *big* things that I shouldn't... [laughter]

Wayne: It doesn't matter if they are big or little. You were suggesting that "shoulds" and "shouldn'ts" are a necessary part of the practical workings of life. I'm saying let's take a look at that. Let's take a look and see if, in fact, what you do *is* a product of that. What you tell me of your experience suggests that that is not necessarily the case. You still do things that run contrary to your values. You still hurt people that you love, even though you know you shouldn't. You still get angry in situations where you know you shouldn't. Why don't you always act in accordance with your values? The question is, are you truly in control of this? That's the question the Living Teaching encourages you to look into.

ADDICTION

Q: About 6 or 8 months ago, I mentioned my issue with drinking, and you said, "Go to AA." Somehow, in my talk with Ramesh, it came up, and he said the same thing, "Go to AA." So I've started going. Intellectually, I seem to understand this teaching, and I just wanted to kind of bounce off of you why in the hell I can't seem to accept the first step of the AA program—that I'm powerless. Part of why I went to India was to attend a 30-day cleansing retreat, where I didn't drink for 30 days, but the minute I got out I started drinking. I can understand that I'm not the author of my actions but I can't seem to accept that I am powerless over this alcohol. I'm just curious if you have any input on that.

Wayne: So if you accept that you're not the author, then where's your problem with powerlessness?

Q: Well I keep thinking, "I can do this, I can do that…"

Wayne: I wish you could hear what you just said. If you're not the author, what do you mean, "I can do this or I can do that"? Obviously the belief that you're not the author is still only an intellectual belief, and that's okay. The first step of AA—that you're powerless over alcohol and your life's unmanageable—is a starting point as well. At first, it is accepted intellectually. If it was completely accepted, one hundred per cent at every level, there would be no need for the next eleven steps. When there is a complete and intuitive Understanding of one's total powerlessness as an individual—that your life is unmanageable by you—which is to say that you're not the author—that is what we call Enlightenment.

~~~

Q: Could the hunger behind any addiction be an expression of the soul searching for something higher?

Wayne: I'm not sure what you mean by "soul." So if we remove that term from the question, and ask, "Could the hunger behind any addiction be an expression of a searching for something higher?" I would say, yes. Addictions are partly a result of an emptiness that is seeking to be filled. However, that which fills it can do so only temporarily, and therefore it continues to be sought. Regardless whether it's a drug or liquor, or if it's sex, or love or God that initially does the trick, the hole is never filled for long. Certain people are addictive by nature, and so what will be a balanced search on the part of one person, will become addictive or obsessive in another. It has to do entirely with the nature of the human organism itself.

WHY AFFLICTION?

Q: What does Consciousness want? In tough times I want to ask, "Consciousness, what do you want of me?" or "Why does Consciousness want to have this experience of difficulty through me?"

Wayne: Your question is rooted in a very heavily dualistic notion that there is an object called Consciousness, and it is separate from this object called you. The pointer of the Living Teaching is that such separation is notional; the separation between you and Consciousness does not actually exist. Consciousness is not a *thing* with desires or agendas relative to *you*. Your question is best answered with an examination of what you truly are. What are you, in relation to Consciousness?

Q: So no motive can be assigned to the functioning of Consciousness?

Wayne: Motives are continuously being attributed to the functioning of Consciousness. The real question is, do those attributions mean anything?

ILLNESS

Q: I have a body that hasn't been cooperating. I have tried many things to change it, or change how I felt about it...

Wayne: Do you have a physical condition of some kind?

Q: Yes. I've had it for a while, and it's become worse. For me to really surrender to the idea that I'm not doing this, that I didn't do anything wrong, has made life incredibly more graceful and easy.

Wayne: I'm absolutely certain of that! And that is one of the great blessings of this Living Teaching, when it finds its mark. A notion that has made its way around the New Age arena for a long time is that you manifest your condition. Thus, if your condition is poor, it means you've done a bad job of manifesting. It falls squarely back into your lap that essentially, you are a screw-up. So, not only are you sick, but you're ultimately responsible for it, too!

Q: Yes, you did something wrong.

Wayne: Right. It's a horrific notion. Normally, I have very little to say about other teachings, but this is one I have a strong aversion to. I just cannot abide this notion that you are in control of your health, you're in control of your condition, and it is within your power to align yourself in the proper way and harmonize with the universe. The implication is inescapable that if you don't do this simple thing, you are an idiot. Furthermore, I can name half a dozen sages who died from cancer. (Though whenever I do, the Health Manifesters simply say that those sages all *chose* to die painful deaths to show us we are not the body.)

The blessing of this Living Teaching is in the understanding that whatever is happening in this moment is the functioning of Totality. Implicit in that understanding is that anything can change at any instant. The fact that something has been happening a certain way until now, does not mean that it's going to persist in that way. Whatever your condition, it's not necessarily going to be this way forever. The very basis of life, the most fundamental element of all that is manifest, is change.

~~~

Q: If a person has bad habits and patterns, can these lead to sickness or some sort of imbalance, like obesity, diabetes, or addictions to drugs and alcohol?

Wayne: They can.

Q: I guess this gets into the question of treatment and therapy. I've seen a lot of great work within this context, where people are getting rid of serious illnesses, not just addictions or stuff like that.

Wayne: Yes, miraculous healings and changes happen all the time. The essential question is: What is the source of the healing? What is the source of the change?

Q: Ah, that's a different perspective.

Wayne: There's no question that people engage in various practices and therapies and there are "positive" results, meaning there are subsequent events that are considered positive. Upon deeper investigation, the causal relationship between the practice and the result gets a little shaky, because there are other people doing the same practice or therapy and they get sicker and die. Absolute causal links are difficult to establish. Try investigating this for yourself.

Q: But the actual source of the healing, that's different. So you're not denying the aspect of being proactive and altering one's condition in a "healthy" way, but rather to what degree one is actually the source of the proactivity. If I cut myself, I am to understand that even if I clean the wound, I'm not actually healing my cut. The Life Force is doing that. Is that what you're referring to?

Wayne: What I'm saying is that you will apply a treatment based on your best information and conditioning. Two hundred years ago, the best treatment would be to bleed the person or apply leeches; physicians would bring about healing through these means, and the College of Surgeons was recommending such practices, having observed that many of their patients recovered.

Today we would look at this same practice and say that after further observation it would seem that the practice is counterproductive. And I'm sure lots of things that we are currently doing will eventually be re-evaluated in the same way. In fact, this morning's paper had an article stating that flu shots for the elderly, previously touted as saving 80% of the lives of people who use them, had been shown in the latest study to have no effect.

We must operate on the basis of what we know. We must, and we do. It's the nature of the human organism to do so. The pointer of this Living Teaching is to expand one's perspective a bit, to understand that our actions are the results of forces greater than our physical-mental-emotional selves.

Q: So even the proactivity is not authored by us?

Wayne: Precisely. Nor is a positive outcome of that proactivity assured.

~~~

Q: If your body became ill, would you do visualization, or would you just go to the doctor?

Wayne: My body *has* become ill, so I can tell you experientially what I've done in the past; I've sometimes gone to the doctor but I have never done visualizations.

Q: Okay.

Wayne: But what I'll do the next time I get sick, I have no way of predicting.

WHO IS SUFFERING?

Q: Is suffering a function of the FSA?

Wayne: Yes, FSA-involvement in What Is produces suffering. The FSA isn't the source of suffering, it is the instrument *through which* suffering is produced. The FSA is actually impotent. It does nothing other than claim. It will claim that it is producing the suffering, because it is in its nature to claim potency. But it's a false claim. If the FSA is absent, then there is no possibility of suffering arising in the organism.

~~~

Q: Buddha said that Enlightenment is the end of suffering. So is that peace?

Wayne: Yes, Enlightenment is the end of suffering. When people hear that statement they often relate it to their own experience of the moment when pain stops, or when there was a period of spiritual revelation. They often say, "I've had that experience, I know what that feels like. The Buddha must be saying Enlightenment is having that experience all the time!" Unfortunately, it's not.

Q: It is the end of FSA involvement?

Wayne: Enlightenment is the end of the FSA itself, not the end of the *involvement*. With the death of the FSA, there is no place from which the involvement can arise. This is completely different than the movement from involvement to non-involvement; an occurrence Ramesh calls "the flip-flop."

Q: How do you know when the FSA is not active?

Wayne: The FSA is not active most of the time. The FSA is, in fact, involved in relatively little of your daily doing. You blink, you digest, you breathe, you have thoughts all through the day, and there is no FSA involvement throughout most of it. What characterizes FSA-involvement is suffering. When the FSA does become involved, there is often a sense of separation or resistance. The suffering can be intense or it can be just a sense of disquiet, of not feeling completely comfortable in your skin, but whatever form it takes, it is a product of FSA-involvement in what is happening.

~~~

Q: There is a part of me that is not accepting the teaching that all my thoughts and my neuroses are God's will operating through me.

Wayne: And so you suffer guilt for your bad thoughts and neuroses. Keep in mind that the non-accepting of that is *also* God's will. This Living Teaching does not tell you that you *should* accept. Rather, it invites you to inquire in the hope that Acceptance may come.

When there is Acceptance, there is peace. When there is non-acceptance, there is suffering. You may begin to associate that which is desirable with God, and that which is not desirable with being human. It's a throwback to the basic split between the spiritual and the material. The pointer of this Living Teaching always goes beyond that spiritual/material split to the underlying unity of both. The spiritual and material are complimentary aspects of the same Essence.

SECTION
EIGHT:
UNIVERSAL CONCERNS

BRINGING ORDER TO THE WORLD

Q: Somebody said that trying to make the world a better place is arrogant and warlike.

Wayne: That was Leonard Cohen. But his precise statement was that the idea that you set the universe "in order" is arrogant and warlike. This doesn't exclude the desire to do something to create a future change, or to help someone. Obviously, your actions to help someone, or to end a conflict, are also part of the functioning of Totality. The arrogance lies in presuming this action you perform is organizing things as they *should* be. That's an incredible presumption on the part of a single human being.

The ultimate humility of the sage is the tacit understanding that "I am an instrument through which Totality functions. What I do, whether people like it or don't like it, whether they approve of it or disapprove of it, is part of What Is." That's not being self-effacing, which is what humility is often thought to be—a self-deprecating "Oh, it was nothing"—because the sage *truly* knows it was not his self-authored act, good or bad. He has the deepest possible conviction that whatever happens is part of the functioning of the Universal Life Force. His is genuine humility.

PROGRESS?

Q: Does it matter if one yearns to evolve, to be—I don't want to say "better"—but somehow more?

Wayne: If you yearn to evolve, it matters for you. For the people who don't yearn to evolve, it doesn't matter. You can say to them, "It's very important for you to yearn to evolve," and they're going to look at you like you're crazy and ask "What do I have to evolve for?"

Q: So, either path is okay.

Wayne: Both *happen*. "Okay" or "not okay" is something that is subsequently put on top of what happens.

HELPING THE WORLD

Q: Does it help the world as a whole, instead of being on the front line fighting the system, to be in meditation and to be in bliss?

Wayne: It depends on who you ask.

Q: It's better for me. I don't know about the world. Is it this vibration that is going to heal the world?

Wayne: I have absolutely no capacity to tell the future. What I'm present with is what's happening. And what is happening at the moment is that we have people fighting on all fronts—violently, passionately, in a variety of ways. Also, in this moment, we have others who are very passive, who are very expansive, who are very open, who are in bliss. Both exist, as part of the functioning of the Source. What will happen next? Who knows? If you believe in trends, then you can make a case for a trend. If you believe in miracles, then you can have faith in a coming miracle. This Living Teaching is solely concerned with What Is and within the What Is there is no limitation.

Q: God expresses through all of us, even those who are fighting, as well as those who are in meditative bliss?

Wayne: Absolutely. That's the model here. Consciousness or God, or Source, is everything. There is only One. Thus, all the permutations of the Oneness are still the Oneness. So, the soldier or the social activist are as much the Oneness as the beatific saint, whose very presence inspires love and generosity in the hearts of all who perceive him or her.

~~~

Q: I have heard that the Transcendental Meditators are getting together—forty thousand or some number—and they are going to turn the world into a peaceful place if they can get enough meditators.

Wayne: I hope it works this time. They never seem to get enough! That's been the problem: if they could just get one more, then it will happen. [laughter] Maybe it will. Maybe they *do* need just one more. I have no way of knowing …!

Q: If we get 51% of people who are aware, who are conscious, would that tip the other 49%?

Wayne: Depends on who you ask. It is currently a popular idea.

Q: I'm asking you.

Wayne: I don't have any answers. And I can't predict the future.

Q: Okay. Then that means I don't have any answers either.

Wayne: If you're lucky!

~~~

Q: How can one deal with the pain of witnessing so much suffering in the world, and the feeling of powerlessness in the face of it?

Wayne: People deal with that pain in a variety of ways. There is no blueprint for dealing with it. Every person deals with it in his or her own way. You can look at your history and see how you have dealt with it in the past, and perhaps you will do that again. If you are a sensitive, empathetic person, then witnessing others' pain is difficult.

Mind you, there are lots of people who blissfully go through their days totally ignorant of the pain of others. It simply doesn't register, and they don't have to deal with it at all. But obviously you're not such a person. Your sensitivity to the pain of others brings about pain in yourself.

Whether or not that pain moves you to some kind of action has to do with your nature. Ramesh used to tell this story all the time about the French actress, Brigitte Bardot. She was watching television, and she saw the baby harp seals being clubbed up in Canada. Hunters were out there clubbing these seals, and these seals are really cute, so to see these things being brutally clubbed was just more than she could bear. She said, "This is horrible! This is an awful thing, absolutely awful!" And she started an organization that eventually put enough pressure on the Canadian government so that the practice was stopped.

Coincidentally, there is another account of the spiritual teacher J. Krishnamurti who was watching a similar program of these baby harp seals being brutally clubbed, and after watching for a few moments he said, "This is horrible, this is unbearable, I can't watch this. Turn that off!" His solution was to turn the television off so that he didn't have to see the offending sight.

Q: It's a beautiful irony that it was the spiritual teacher who looked away and the actress who did something.

Wayne: The story is without judgment about either one of them. It was meant to point to how we are all programmed differently. The nature of one organism was to act to bring about a change. The nature of the other organism, in that situation, was to simply re-move the offending vision from his sight. In a different situation, the teacher might act in a way we would consider admirable and the actress might not act at all.

~~~

Q: I work to restore natural ecological communities. Am I doing Gaia's work or simply being self-righteous?

Wayne: The question that this Living Teaching asks is how is it that Jim does what Jim does? Is Jim doing Jim's will, or is Jim doing the will of the Source? That is a question that Jim has to find out for himself. Is Jim the source of what he does, or is Jim an instrument through which the Source functions, in this case, with the intention to restore ecological communities? Other organisms are apparently created to destroy ecological communities. How is it that Jim is doing the constructive work and some other organism is doing the destructive work? If you investigate this within yourself, you might be surprised at the insight that comes.

GIVING UP THE WORLD

Q: There's a temptation to go after spiritual states rather than the Natural State, which is, of course, Nothing.

Wayne: Exactly, so I am a big fan of going for whatever moves you—it could be sex, it could be chocolate, it could be helping others, it could be spiritual unity—it doesn't matter to me what it is, but if you're passionately drawn to something, I say go for it—enjoy, live!

Q: Well, I recognize that it's just another object, so it hardly seems worth pursuing.

Wayne: Look at what you just said: "It's *just* another object," so it's hardly worth bothering with. What I'm saying is that *all* the objects are the expressions of the Totality. They're not "just another object," they are God incarnate! So if you want to know God, *there* it is! Enlightenment is not out there in void-land.

Q: Well I would have thought it would be better to go within and to dis-identify with all the stuff of life, rather than to seek God in objects.

Wayne: It's a common conviction that only Consciousness is worthwhile, and all objects are merely illusions and, therefore, beneath contempt. What the Living Teaching points at, over and over again, is that all there is, is Consciousness. All of the objects, even if they are chimeras, are Consciousness. You and him and her and me and the computer, and the chair and the waterfall and the fish, are Consciousness. *Everything* is Consciousness, and nothing is any more Consciousness than anything else. So when you say to go within, go within what? What is that which you would go within, other than Consciousness?

Q: Ramana Maharshi said the Self is like a screen and the objects are shadows playing upon the screen, and one should be more focused on the screen.

Wayne: That was a potent teaching image in Ramana's time because the whole notion of motion pictures was magical—Southern India in the 30s and 40s—this was unbelievable stuff. So this image that he used, of life playing out on the screen of Consciousness, was very powerful. The problem comes because you inevitably objectify Consciousness as a separate thing, in relation to the images playing out upon it.

The initial thrust of the Living Teaching is to shake loose this notion of the FSA being in control of things. To do this, it encourages you to challenge the assumption that you are the source of your thoughts, feeling and actions. Ramana would say, "The Source is much greater than you, you are simply an image played out upon the screen of Totality." But in the next instant, he'd come forth with a totally non-dual pointer suitable for seekers with a more mature understanding.

GOOD AND EVIL

Q: You keep saying, "It is all spiritual." I have a little trouble with that. I always imagine a murderer walking into my house with a gun pointing at my son or daughter. It is very difficult for me to call that spiritual.

Wayne: It *is* difficult. It demands you expand your definition of what is spiritual beyond what you like, beyond what seems right to you, to include the most horrific things imaginable. Everything must be understood to be an aspect of What Is. The Living Teaching invites you to consider that everything— good and bad, what you like and don't like, that which hurts your heart and that which expands your heart— is a product of the same Source.

We're conditioned from childhood with the notion that God is only the good. The bad is suggested to be the work of some other force. In many religions, human beings are said to be the source of the bad. This gives rise to the notion that you must get rid of the human qualities to be more like God. This very basic notion infuses many cultures: God is the big, perfect thing, and that which is earthbound and mundane is sullied, tarnished or dirty.

What I found so expansive about Ramesh's teaching is that it broadened the scope of what was godly and what was spiritual. When he used the term Totality, he really meant it. This Totality is actually total; it includes everything. The bad, the ugly, the murderers, the torturers, the child molesters—all of the horrors—are also included in the Totality that is God.

The acceptance of this Totality being what it is, does not preclude the human response. You're programmed as an instrument to respond in a human way. If somebody comes in and points a gun at you,

you'll respond according to your programming. You may run or make a counterattack; you'll act in accordance with whatever your nature is in that moment. This Acceptance I talk about is not passivity; it places no limit on action or response. It includes every imaginable response.

INTELLECTUAL UNDERSTANDING

Q: Is it part of our intellect to try to figure out what life means?

Wayne: Some intellects are interested in such questions. We generally call those people seekers after knowledge, or seekers after truth. They want to know; they want to understand. The path of knowledge is one of the traditional yogic paths. Certain types of human organisms are drawn to that kind of seeking. There are other kinds of seeking as well. Devotional, heart-centered seeking is one type, and active, doing seeking is another. Different people are physically and temperamentally suited for different paths.

WHAT MATTERS? TO WHOM?

Q: Why does my awareness keep changing?

Wayne: Because whatever is manifest changes. Anything that is manifest is in movement.

The manifest universe—from the most elemental atomic structure to the vastest galactic structure—is in constant movement. It's always changing. Change is the fundamental building block of the manifest world.

Q: The energy is just doing what it does?

Wayne: Clearly, energy's doing what it does. In this Living Teaching, the term Consciousness represents all there is. All there is, is Consciousness.

Q: What can we do about it anyhow?

Wayne: The question really is, to whom does it matter? Obviously, things matter. But they only matter from the personal perspective. Something that matters to you may not matter to her, and vice versa. The point is if it matters to you, it matters. Mattering means something is significant and important. You care.

Q: Is it really nothing other than just a fluctuation?

Wayne: Well, look for yourself. Something that matters today doesn't matter tomorrow. In your own history, there was stuff that was keeping you awake six months ago that you cannot even remember today. It mattered in that moment. It was significant. It was perhaps the biggest thing in your life. Today, it does not matter at all. So, what does that tell you about the mattering?

~~~

Q: It seems that the FSA is a meaning machine. It creates meaning, generates meaning.

Wayne: What you are describing is the activity of the mind, not the FSA. The mind is a meaning machine. The organism cannot function unless it gives meaning to things. Meaning is synonymous with significance. A word has meaning or it doesn't. If it doesn't have a meaning, you cannot communicate with it; you can't use it. If you pick up a tool and you don't know what it does, it doesn't have any meaning for you, so you can't use it. Meaning is essential for the functioning of the organism.

In my model, the FSA only claims. It doesn't actually do anything. The FSA does not provide significance, does not bring about anything. It simply claims involvement or authorship for what is happening, including the mind which gives meaning to events.

UNIVERSE IS NOT HUMAN-HEARTED

Q: Are all the good things and bad things in life just illusions of the mind?

Wayne: They are evaluations by the mind. What we consider to be good is inevitably so only from the human perspective. One of the most devastating things I ever heard Ramesh say is that the universe is not human-hearted. When he said it, in that particular moment, it hit the target completely. I really saw it—totally saw it. Yes, the universe is universal. It includes everything. And humanity is an infinitesimal aspect of that whole.

Q: But isn't the universe a concept as well? Even matter and energy are just concepts. Stating that the universe is not human-hearted ends up being a notion too. Aren't we just spinning around in the end, no "real" point to make, at play with concepts?

Wayne: And that's where we ask, *who* cares? You say, "no real point." *Who* cares whether or not there's a real point? Is there something real that cares or doesn't care? They may well be notions, they may well be concepts, but for whom is it significant or insignificant? That is the very essence of the Living Teaching. I can understand your desire to throw out all these concepts and say nothing's real, it's all illusion. But who or what is operative here?

Q: The hard part of this is that there's no one here to know or understand, yet the seeing needs to be done without the seer. Which means you're left with this.

Wayne: And what is this that you're left with? And how do you relate to it? Are you not part of this? If you don't exist, who cares? [laughter] There is no one here to be Enlightened but there IS Enlightenment here.

HOW DID WE GET SO SCREWED UP?

Q: How did we all get so screwed up? It seems that everyone identifies as a separate entity, when in reality we are not separate from one another. How is it that billions and billions of people are so caught up, and feel so separate?

Wayne: This is described in Ramesh's phrase "the Divine hypnosis." It is really a lovely image. This hypnosis is Divinely placed, meaning that it is not that "we" screwed up. It is not that we fell from grace through some mistake on our part, starting with eating the apple in the Garden of Eden. Religions have promulgated that notion for millennia; it's good for business, but that has no place within this Living Teaching.

In this Living Teaching, the understanding is that Consciousness is everything, including this sense of separation. It clearly is part of the drama of human life. Most human life is integrally connected to the sense of personal authorship and the sense of separation.

Q: If I were creating the universe, I would do it differently.

Wayne: You're going to have to make your suggestions directly to God about how things might better be constructed. I'm solely concerned with pointing to the nature of What Is.

~~~

Q: What about when other people are involved, when you know you are hurting other people?

Wayne: Yes, you may well be the instrument through which pain is caused to others, and often that doesn't feel good. It doesn't feel good if these are people you like, that you care about. So, how is it that even though you don't want to, you sometimes behave in such a way that brings pain to those that you love and care about and thus bring pain back upon yourself? If you become curious about this, it is potentially one of the most fruitful areas of investigation.

~~~

Q: I want to get out of my own way so that I feel that connection, that universal connection, but it feels so far away sometimes. There's this constant yearning, and fear of the intensity of it, fear of the surrender to it.

Wayne: Well, perhaps with a little luck we could shine some light onto the nature of this yearning for unity and connection. Perhaps we'll reveal the nature of that sense that "you" are in the way, that either through "your" fear or through some other means, "you" are creating this problem, and that if "you" just get your act together, then "you" can un-create the problem. Perhaps, we will see if that is actually the case. Are you truly the source of the problem? Are you the source of the separation in the first place? Or are you, as this person, the instrument through which a separation and a yearning happens?

If you are, in fact, the source of the separation, then *stop it!* [hitting chair] Don't do that anymore! Simply stop, then everything will work out fine! But you have undoubtedly tried to stop without success. So what must that mean?

Once you begin to see you are not the source of the separation, then that enormous load of having to stop it starts to ease. Yes, the yearning is there; yes, the feeling of separation is there; and yes, sometimes the feeling of unity is there as well. There is no question that the feeling of unity is preferable to the feeling of separation.

But when we remove this burden of responsibility that it is up to you to manipulate yourself and the rest of the universe into getting more of the unity and less of the separation, life becomes much more peaceful. Even the unpleasantness of the separation becomes less onerous when you no longer feel that the separation is somehow your fault, that you've lost the magic key because you've somehow screwed up.

This Living Teaching encourages you to look to see if the separation that you experience is your doing, or if it is part of a larger happening. The Living Teaching contains no doctrine that says this is how it is or that our way is the right way to perceive things. Rather, the Living Teaching invites you to look for yourself: are you the source of your own discomfort? Are you the source of the original yearning? Are you the source of the separation that creates the yearning?

Did you one day decide to be separate, to leave the blissful state of unity that you were born with and existed in until you were about two-and-a-half years old? Did you at two-and-a-half decide, "Things are going much too smoothly here, I think I'll mess with it, so I can experience separation and begin suffering." Is that a choice you made to create the separation and then live with the suffering that attends it?

Don't accept anyone else's answers. Look into it for yourself. This Living Teaching contains numerous concepts and ideas. Their value is not in what they represent, but in what they may propel you to do; hopefully, to look, to see—and with Grace—to Understand this most fundamental Truth of what you actually Are.

THE END IS THE BEGINNING

As of this writing (June 2009) Wayne Liquorman is traveling the world, sharing his Living Teaching in talks, seminars and retreats. If you have found the contents of this book to be of interest and would like to meet Wayne, details of his schedule can be found on the Advaita Fellowship website:

www.advaita.org

The Advaita Fellowship
P.O. Box 3479 EN
Redondo Beach, CA 90277
USA

Tel. 310-376-9636

More From Advaita Press

A Duet of One by Ramesh S. Balsekar

Here Ramesh uses the Ashtavakra Gita as a vehicle for an illuminating look at the nature of duality and dualism.
Softcover 224 Pages $16.00

Who Cares?! by Ramesh S. Balsekar

This is the boook we recommend to those asking for a book that will describe the essence of Ramesh's teaching. Ramesh's ability to cut through to the simple heart of complex ideas is a joy to experience.
Softcover 220 Pages $16.00

Acceptance of What IS by Wayne Liquorman

A look at Advaita through the eyes of the most unlikely of Sages. Wayne's expression of his spiritual understanding is at once irreverent and profound. We laugh, sometimes joyously, sometimes uncomfortably but always with the recognition that we are in the presence of a Master.
Softcover 304 Pages $16.00

Your Head In The Tiger's Mouth by Ramesh S. Balsekar

A superb overview of the Teaching. Transcribed portions of talks Ramesh gave in his home in Bombay during 1996 and 1997.
Softcover 472 Pages $24.00

A Net Of Jewels by Ramesh S. Balsekar

A handsome bedside volume of jewels of Advaita, selections from Ramesh's writings presented in the format of twice daily meditations. Hardcover 384 Pages $25.00

Never Mind by Wayne Liquorman
Take a revealing and inspiring journey into the heart of Non-Duality. Wayne's Teaching is presented here with clarity and sophistication. *A most welcome addition to the spiritual library.* Softcover 174 Pages $17.00

Ripples by Ramesh S. Balsekar

A brief and concise introduction to Ramesh's Teaching. Perfect to give to friends.   Softcover 44 Pages $6.00

SEE NEXT PAGE FOR ORDERING DETAILS

NO WAY *for the spiritually advanced* by Ram Tzu

 No Way is a unique blending of wit, satire and profound spiritual insight. One minute we are howling with unconstrained laughter, the next we are squirming in self-conscious recognition as Ram Tzu holds up a perfect mirror and then gleefully points out that we aren't wearing any clothes.
Softcover - 112 Pages $13.00
Also available on Audio Cassette $15.00

===============

If unavailable at your bookstore, these titles and many others may be ordered directly from the Advaita Press Store at **www.advaita.org**

OR

Send check, money order or Visa/Mastercard or American Express number (include expiration date and billing zip code) for the indicated amount plus shipping as noted below to:

Advaita Press
P.O. Box 3479 EN
Redondo Beach, CA 90277
USA

Shipping & Handling:

In U.S. :
  Surface mail: First book $5.50. Add $1.00 each additional.
  Airmail: First book $7.75. Add $1.00 each additional book.

Outside U.S.Å.:
  Canada Airmail: First Book $9.00. Add $4.00 each additional.
  International Airmail: $12.00 per book.
  International Surface mail: $7.00 per book

Payment in U.S. dollars via credit card, check or money order payable on a U.S. bank. No Eurochecks please.

www.advaita.org